Clare and its people

— a concise history —

by

Brian Dinan

THE MERCIER PRESS
CORK and DUBLIN

Dedicated to
my mother Eileen Morgan and my father John Dinan R.I.P
and for
Michael Morgan

A special word of thanks to my wife

ELIZABETH

whose love and forbearance (not to mention many typings of the MSS)
sustained me in completing the book.

British Library Cataloguing in Publication Data

Dinan, Brian
    Clare and its people.
1. Clare — Social life and customs
I. Title
941.9'3   DA990.C59
ISBN 0-85342-828-X

The Mercier Press, 4 Bridge Street, Cork.
24 Lower Abbey Street, Dublin 1.
© Brian Dinan 1987
ISBN 085342 828 X

Printed by Litho Press Co., Midleton, Co. Çork.

CONTENTS

ACKNOWLEDGEMENT

The author wishes to acknowledge the courtesy and services of the staff of both the Clare County Library and the Limerick County Library and Sean Spellisy, without whom the publication of this work would not be possible.
The author and publisher would also like to thank the National Library of Ireland, the Office of Public Works, Shannon Development, the ESB, and The Illustrated London News Picture Library for permission to use their photographs.

FOREWORD

Some time ago while browsing in the splendid Ennis library, I came across a number of reference works on the history of Clare. From that moment on I became fascinated by the Dalcassian clans, their wars, their castles, their villains and their heroes. I remember thinking what a pity it was that access to reference works by the public was somewhat restricted because of time constraints, and because of the difficulty of wading through heavy matter to find just what one is looking for.

Such was my enthusiasm for the Dalcassians after my sojourn in the library, that I began at every available opportunity to make known to my friends the doings and deeds of the Dalcassian clans. When I found it difficult at times to recall accurate detail to amuse my friends, I thought how much better it would be if all of that great story were compiled in one concise history which the layman could glide through without drudgery. My research began through numerous sources and from it was born this complete little history of Clare and its people.

It was my intention at the outset to achieve three main objectives: outline a complete story from first inhabitants up to the modern day; produce a readable work rather than a scholarly one; retain the fascination from other reference works which would make interesting reading for the modern Clare man and woman. If I succeed in the above I will be pleased indeed. Perhaps the book will inspire some fresh efforts from other Dalcassians. If it does I will be doubly pleased.

So, dear reader, step away from the gadgetry of the twentieth century and return with me through the veil of time. Let's go back to those first tentative steps of ancient man in our county, to our beginnings in this part of the world. Let us battle through forest, hunger and enemies alike with our proud forebearers. Indeed let us relive our historic past — and see then do we return to the present century as the same man or woman who took time out to be curious about our history.

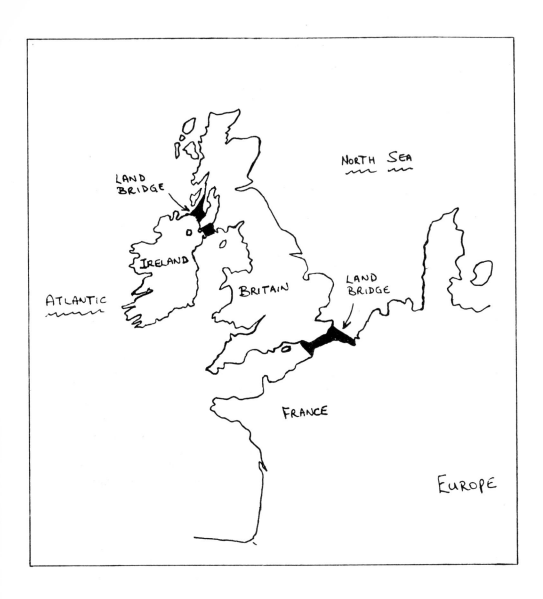

Map shows land bridges between Ireland, Britain and the Continent. Animals migrated in this way from Europe through Britain into Ireland.

Chapter 1

Formation and First Settlers
(Earliest times — 1000 BC)

The formation of this country and with it the present county of Clare, goes back to the dawn of civilisation. We must return to the Ice Age to trace those formations and beginnings.

The most recent Ice Age occurred about the time of the Pleistocene Epoch which began about 1¾ million years ago and finished about 10,000 years ago.

As the great ice cap melted and receded northwards from the continent of Europe it exposed the high land masses that we now call Britain and Ireland. The melting ice mass scraped the land as it slid towards the seas, gouging out lakes and fjords. It also deposited boulders, clay and sand in many places. The result of this activity is much in evidence around County Clare where huge boulders can be found. High sand dunes can be seen in places like Lahinch, Fanore and Doolin. The exposed northern cap of Clare, the Burren, has almost been scraped clean of soil by the retreating ice cap.

Before the ice cap had fully retreated to its present position (due to increasing temperatures), the seas were lower than they are now. Land bridges connected Ireland to Scotland, also Britain to the continent of Europe. Those bridges allowed the migration of animals into Ireland, thus explaining the presence of the great Irish elk and other animals now extinct, when the first settlers later arrived by canoe. It was the final ice melting which was responsible for raising the ocean levels to cover the existing English Channel and the land link to present-day Scotland.

It is known that at 10,000 BC the great elk, wolves, bears and wild boar existed in what was then a wooded fertile island. In the caves of Edenvale and Newhall (near Ennis) numerous bones of the bear have been found. Some of them seem to have been subjected to stewing or cooking.

It is also known that early primitive man often followed the movement of animals. He relied on their skins for clothing, their meat for food and their bones for use as working tools. Whether or not early man was in Ireland at that time we cannot be sure. What we do know is that Neolithic Stone Age Man was in Ireland at some stage of the period in question. We know this because traces of his existence have been found in the Stone Age implements that he used.

One of the most sought-after pieces of stone by Neolithic man was undoubtedly flint. Flint abounded, exposed, in large quantities off the north-east coast of County Antrim. After the land bridges were covered by ocean waters, Stone Age man crossed from Scotland in skin clad boats to the coast of Antrim. They were perhaps the first real inhabitants of Ireland.

In time, those first inhabitants of the country spasmodically sailed around the island coastline and up the river inlets. The approximate date of their arrival would have been around 5,000 BC. It is thought that they were of the Campignian culture and came from the Mediterranean basin. Legend has it that they came from an area of Greece, where they were enslaved as landworkers. Their tasks included shifting large quantities of earth in sacks to fertilise the land of their masters. Hence, they have been given the name Firbolg, or Bagmen.

The Campignian culture is a reference to the state of archaeological development at the time we refer to, and is identified by primitive flint working tools which would be analogous with 25-foot beach sites in Ireland and Scotland. Essentially, people of this culture were mainly familiar with flint as working tools. Stone hand axes would also be included in this culture.

It is easy then to envisage small numbers of hide-covered canoes, containing Neolithic Stone Age man, advancing up the Shannon estuary. The occupants of those flimsy craft included men, women and children. They would have peered apprehensively beyond the mudflats to the jungle-like forestry all around them. Although they knew that the shorelines were inhabited by their own kind, they were fearful of what they might encounter in the interior.

The people themselves were low and squat in size, almost aboriginal in appearance. Their complexions were swarthy, and their forms were both thick and strong. They wore rough clothes of animal hide and they were not accustomed to many comforts. Metals were unknown to them, but they did carry crude instruments of flint and polished stone. With their primitive tools they worked hides into clothes. Spears and axes of stone were used for hunting down the wild boar.

As proof of their existence, they left behind on the shores of Clare lumps of fine clay as would be used in the making of pottery. A flint digger has been found in a dried lake-bed near Scariff and some stone implements were unearthed in Fisher Street (Doolin) on the west coast. Also left behind were piles of shells from oysters, mussels, cockles and periwinkles. These they threw in heaps when they had finished feasting on them.

Initially, they lived in small wooden huts. Later they built small round stone structures, which looked like large beehives. Traces of these can still be found today. For a long time Neolithic man stayed close to the coastline. When he became established in coastal settlements, his next venture was inland in canoes via the waterways.

The wide estuaries of the Shannon and Fergus proved inviting to those first inhabitants. It was possible for them to paddle many miles upriver and still have an escape route to the sea, should they have met powerful foes, either human or animal. In time, groups of these people specialised in living along the river estuaries, just as others did on the sea shores. The people who worked the shallows or estuaries became classified as Riverford Culture. They would have become adept at such food gathering techniques as selecting and clearing riverside vegetation, erecting weirs and traps to catch salmon at the time of migration. One study tells us that the Riverford people were advanced in stone-working tools and seemed to avoid flint. This was an advance on the Beachcombers — those people who first gathered food from our shores. It appears that the Riverford people were the predecessors of the Megalithic builders.

By using their highly navigable canoes as a means of transport, it is likely that Neolithic man came to where Clarecastle and Ennis now stand. Over the centuries, they, and others like them who came to this island, gradually populated (albeit sparsely) the entire country. When they first came they were hunters and food gatherers. Later, with their rough stone implements they managed to clear small areas of fertile ground in which to grow their crops. In time, having moved inland, they became our first farmers.

Even though the Firbolg were in loose possession of the island for many years, they were not left undisturbed. Occasional small migrations almost certainly took place. The most noteworthy of these would undoubtedly have been the arrival of the African sea rovers, the Fomorians. Apparently, their main stronghold was off the north-west coast on Tory island.

Recent investigations into Irish links with North Africa seem to suggest that in fact such a people as the Fomorians could be the ancestors of some of the present-day Irish. Irish music (present-day traditional) and sean-nós singing bear a remarkable similarity to that of the people in some North African countries today. Since traditional music is very strong in the County of Clare it is possible that we may have derived at least a small part of our heritage from the Fomorian influence.

Later still, well into the Bronze Age, would come a similar people, namely the mythical race of magic and wizardry — the Tuatha De Danann (people of the Goddess Danu). It is presumed that the Tuatha De Dannan were also referred to as the Sword People. With their bronze swords they easily succeeded in wresting control of the country from the existing primitive people.

This they did firstly, against the Firbolg on the Mayo-Galway border. Later they repeated their success with another great victory over the second tribe in the country, the Formorians. This second battle took place at northern Moytura, in Galway.

The De Danann were a unique people, uncommonly skilled in the arts of those times. Even the Milesians, who later conquered them, regarded them as magicians. Some of their skills became immortalised in the legends of the Milesians who were to arrive in the country later on.

After these battles, the De Danann were the undisputed masters of the land. However, the country continued to be populated by large numbers of Firbolg who were then subjected to a life of serfdom. This situation pertained until the arrival of the Milesians.

The entire country at that time was covered in huge primeval forests, interspersed with pine and great oaks. Near where Ennis now stands, the river Fergus spread delta-like on the flat lush landscape. It meandered through this soft marshy spot, some of which can still be seen at the rear of the Convent of Mercy at Clonroad.

Many bands of Firbolg, and later De Danann, found this an ideal location to settle in safety for awhile. By camping on the island, they were safely surrounded by the river or the treacherous marshes. Not being a people given to constructing large stone fortifications, they could not as individual groups hold permanent vantage points for very long. This location (and indeed any other location in the county) would not be urbanised to any great extent by the Firbolg or De Danann. Their lack of intricate organisation on a large scale saw to that.

This delta-like spot in the central plains of Clare was at that time sur-

Unique limestone surface in the Burren.

rounded with thick forestry which was infested with wolves and boar. A thirty mile radius can be described with Ennis as the centre, which would take in most of the present county. This spot proved to be the natural administration pivot for both military and civil rulers. This was the case down the centuries. It was the heart of Clare.

To the east of the river delta at Ennis stand the Ogonnoloe and Broadford Hills. Their round rugged summits guard Lough Derg and the majestic Shannon river. This great waterway forms the eastern and southern boundaries of the county until it reaches the tidal estuary at Limerick.

Barren peaty ranges of open land, often lashed by raging storms, cover the county's western extremity. To the north-west, a unique one hundred and sixty square miles of flat limestone landscape — the Burren — was always much in evidence as it is today.

With the Shannon to the east and south, the wild Atlantic to the west; the hills of Feakle, Glendree and O'Dea Hills forming a northerly division with Galway, it makes a unique peninsular tract of territory with ideal natural boundaries. It was to this area that the old tribes would be pushed by the new invader.

The Firbolg were dominant in Ireland for nearly three thousand years before the birth of Christ. They, in turn, were dominated by the De Danann for some centuries until the Celts landed. From then on both races were reduced to a lower existence by the latest invader.

The Firbolg lived a harsh life. They cleared small patches of land by hacking at the trees and undergrowth with bronze and stone tools. Crops grown at that time were corn and edible green plants mainly. They gained much of their food from nature by killing deer, boar and fish, and eating wild nuts and berries. The women folk spent their day grinding corn with quern stones and spinning a rough wool thread from sheep's hide.

Their homes consisted of cramped structures made from timber, pliable hazel and mud. It was customary for them to live in inaccessible marshy wastelands, or on elevated ground. Their main fear was of being attacked by wolves, who were both plentiful and vicious. The wolf made travel through the forest a very dangerous expedition indeed.

During this period, (2000 BC to 350 BC) in the Bronze Age, a number of ringed forts were built. Some were used as burial grounds, more were residential and others could simply have been used as cattle pens. The more elaborate and better-known ring forts in the county would have been constructed after the Bronze Age by the Celts themselves. One of the finest circular earthen forts can be found about a mile from Killaloe.

We can thank the pre-Celtic people for the many Megalithic tombs, or dolmens, scattered about the county. They seem to have been built at the end of the Stone Age, about four thousand years ago. It would appear that they were constructed in memory of dead kings and chieftains. A thick belt of these dolmens runs across Clare and part of Limerick. They are always most common near the coast and alongside large rivers.

Perhaps one of the most famous of these dolmens in Clare, if not in Ireland, is Poulnabrone in the Burren. This type of tomb is rare and is more accurately described as a portal-tomb, dating from the Neolithic period (prior to 2000

Poulnabrone Dolmen in the Burren.

BC). Its construction has withstood the test of time for at least four thousand years, although recent inspections revealed a crack in one of the slabs. This is currently being made safe by repair work.

Clare has more than its fair share of Megalithic tombs. The first survey in the country on these type of structures was carried out in the county. The study, *Megalithic Tombs of Ireland* (De Valera and Ó Nualláin, 1961) is available as a result of this survey.

Megalithic tombs had more than one function for our ancient ancestors. They were used for the worship of gods in human and animal form; for sacrifice (of man, animal and vegetable); fertility rites in crops, animal and man; and as an assembly area for religious ceremonies, song, dance, processions and for the commemoration of the dead.

There is a double court-cairn at Cohaw. This is a particularly fine example of this type of cairn, and it seems as if two single cairns have been placed back-to-back. It consists of semi-circular forecourts at each end with five burial chambers in them. A Stone Age piece of pottery was also found during excavations in 1949.

A box-like megalithic tomb with six upright stones supporting two small capstones can be seen at Ballyhickey. This construction is common to many other tombs found in the county, except for one unusual feature, it has an almost perfectly square shape.

Easy access may be gained from the main road to the wedge-shaped chamber of five standing stones supporting two capstones — the gallery grave at Cahernaphuca. The capstones are more elevated at one end than the other, probably because the method of construction was responsible for this feature, and for no other reason.

Ancient gods of light were worshipped by the pre-Celtic people, and were represented to them in tall stone monoliths. Very often the central figure was surrounded by rings of smaller stones — in acknowledgement of lesser gods. Many of their customs carried over into the early Celtic period, as some of the Firbolg and many of the De Danann were contemporary with the Celts. They therefore imparted some of their habits and culture to the new people.

Two remaining types of marks left by Stone Age and Bronze Age man are cists and standing stones. Cists are box-like small chambers constructed of stone slabs, normally six in number. In addition there would also be a slab floor and slab roof. Generally, they were used to store the cremated bodies of the dead. Many included wordly goods like cups and urns and sometimes weapons. Possibly, the most common remains of antiquity in Ireland are the large single standing stones. The average height of these is eight to twelve feet with some extending to twenty feet at the most. Many of them are memorials for Bronze Age graves but because they are without markings, and lack peculiarity of construction, it is always difficult to date them and to assign significance to them.

Dolmens generally consisted of two or more upright stones supporting a near horizontal slab. Generally the trilithons form part of a larger ensemble of dolmens. Supporting this theory is the fact that there are only three trilithons standing in isolation in the whole of the country, one of these at Mount Callan in Clare.

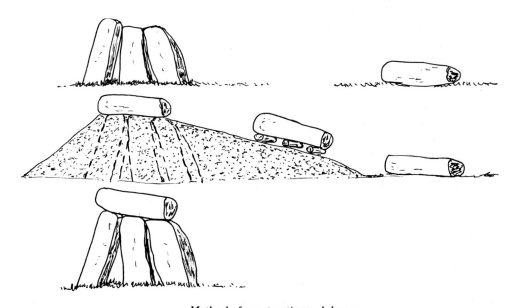

Method of constructing a dolmen.

(Reproduced courtesy of Methuen & Co. from The Archaeology of Ireland by R.A.S. MacAlister).

The method of construction is relatively obvious when the level of sophistication of those times is considered. The upright stones were first embedded in position in the ground. A ramp of rubble and flat stones was built to allow rolling (on logs) or dragging the horizontal stone into position. The ramp material was later removed.

At about 1000 BC, Clare in common with the rest of Ireland, was populated by a people relying on stone and bronze tools. Although their numbers in the country were considerable, they were without sophisticated fortifications of any kind. Their hovels were only a defence against the natural enemy. They were ill-prepared for the men of iron.

Present-day state of a Megalithic Tomb.
Location: North Clare.

Chapter 2

Milesians — Celtic Ancestors (350 BC — AD 432)

At 1000 BC (about the same time as King Solomon reigned in Israel) a Celtic tribe of people were being jostled about in Europe. They found it difficult to settle on a final resting spot, because of pressure from Roman, Greek and German races. They had heard that there was gold to be found in a wonderful land called Hibernia. It seemed like their destiny so they decided on a military expedition to this land that promised wealth and happiness. These people were well accustomed to sea travel and to living dangerously. By using such weapons as heavy iron swords, they had become experienced fighters and much feared adversaries. They were also known as miners and agriculturists and were accomplished in working iron tools and weapons. In long crafts they set sail to conquer the island of Ireland.

It is thought that the main expedition, for there appears to have been more than one, was led by Eber and Eremon, the sons of Mil. The Celts differed from the Firbolg and other existing tribes in Ireland in that they were taller, of fair hair and complexion, and for the most part had blue eyes.

One description given of the Celts by a Roman historian, Diodorus Siculus, went as follows:

> The Gauls (meaning Celtic people) are tall in stature and their flesh is very moist and white, while their hair is not only naturally blond, but they also use artificial means to increase this natural quality of colour. For they continually wash their hair with lime — wash and draw it back from their foreheads to the crown and to the nape of the neck, with the result that their appearance resembles that of Satyrs or Pans, for the hair is so thickened by this treatment that it differs in no way from a horse's mane. Some shave off the beard; the nobles shave the cheeks but let the moustache grow freely so that it covers the mouth. And so when they are eating the moustache becomes entangled in the food, and when they are drinking the drink passes, at it were, through a sort of strainer ...

It was said that the Celts were great talkers and storytellers, even boastful as well. To the Roman observer their appearance was terrifying, with deep-sounding and very harsh voices. They seemed to have used few words in conversation and spoke in riddles, for the most part hinting at things and leaving a great deal to be understood. They were given to frequent exaggeration with the aim of extolling themselves and diminishing the status of others. They are boasters and threateners, said Diodorus Siculus, and given to bombastic self-dramatisation, and yet they are quick of mind and with good natural ability for learning. So, it would appear that the Milesians (as the descendants of Mil became known) who came to Ireland were strong and warlike in the Celtic tradition and meant to impose their will on the island they invaded.

There is very little agreement as to their exact landing place. Some sources say that Eremon and his followers landed at Inver Culpa on the river Boyne in the east of the country. Eber and his survivors beached at Inver Sceine in Bantry Bay, Co Cork. It is probable that the leaders landed in the places mentioned, but also there would have been continuing expeditions arriving in many locations right up to a few centuries AD.

Another variation on how the Celts may have got here is given in the following account: After the Celts were driven from central Europe by Greek, Roman and German tribes, a breakaway group settled in Asia Minor. This territory was called at that time Galatia (modern western Turkey) — remember Paul's epistle to the Galatians. It was named after them — the Gaels. It is thought that they came to Ireland through Egypt, Crete and Spain. They were called Gaedhal (Gael) because their remote ancestor, in the days of Moses, was named Gaedhal Glas. The story goes that Moses cured Gaedhal Glas when a child, of a serpent bite. He promised that no serpent would inhabit the happy western isle that destiny would allow his descendants to inhabit. Niul, his grandson, married a Pharaoh's daughter called Scotia — Ireland in later years was called Scotia. After some time Niul and his tribe were driven from Egypt and eventually sojourned in Spain after long wanderings. They had heard of the western isle, Eireland, took it to be the isle of destiny foretold by Moses long ago and set sail on their voyage of destiny.

Legend has it that their initial attempts to land were thwarted by the wizardy of the De Danann who raised up a sea storm against them. Great numbers of their followers were reputedly lost at sea.

When the Milesians, or Celts, landed, they won their first victory over the De Danann who were being led by Queen Eire. Their own Queen Scotia was lost in the fray. On this very first encounter the bronze blades of the Firbolg (who would have been fighting under directions from the De Danann) were chopped to pieces by the flashing iron blades of the tall fair-haired warriors. It is not inconceivable that the Firbolg and the De Danann administration would have turned in total confusion. The leaders gradually surrendered their local kingdoms to the mighty invader. It was quickly learned throughout the land that bronze could not stand against iron. In a short space of time, the Celts had established themselves as rulers in those divisions of territory previously held by the De Danann and worked by the Firbolg.

Because they had come on quasi-military expeditions it is likely that few women were brought along on the initial assaults. They would, perhaps, have followed on when beach heads were established. Although in this connection it must be remembered that the women of the time were not as dainty as their present day sisters. Indeed they often had considerable power under Brehon Law and were known to have caused and taken part in many a squabble. After the Celts had settled into the country a number of them would have taken local women as wives and consequently some of the native customs were blended in with their own.

With their tempered iron implements they succeeded in clearing large tracts of land for agricultural use. It was a skill at which they were quite adept. They used the local labour in the form of the serfs, mainly Firbolgs, for many purposes. Principally, they put them to work building crannógs and reporting for military service as required.

It is believed that it was the Milesians who first introduced the smelting of gold to Ireland. They initiated the custom of wearing gold ornaments as well as gold fringes on their dress. Generally, the Celts wore simple but colourful clothing, made from linen and woollen materials which they produced themselves. Tunics and long cloaks were popular which were fastened at the neck with pins or brooches. Jewellery was extremely prevalent, and ornaments made from gold such as bracelets, torcs, brooches, pins and gold braided garments were commonly worn by the nobles. Kings and various classes of people were distinguished by the particular colours on their dress. A king and a queen would wear seven colours; a poet or an ollamh was allowed six; a chieftain, five; an army commander, four; local landowners were authorised three colours; a rent payer, two; and a serf only one.

The construction of ringed forts (particularly stone forts) continued in this period and indeed were expanded and improved upon right into the Christian era. In the Burren area the remnants of some stone forts can be observed today. There is a particularly interesting one at Cahercommaun. It is situated at the edge of a steep valley. In construction it resembles Dun Aengus on the Aran Islands, with three concentric walls all abutting a steep cliff edge. During the Harvard Archaeological Expedition to Ireland in 1934 it was discovered that the enclosure contained a dozen stone buildings dating from different periods. A silver brooch was found in one of the souterrains, but no history could be attached to the structure itself.

Not far from Cahercommaun is a fort called Cashlaun Gas. It is difficult to find, being much overgrown and partially concealed on a flat hilltop with a sheer drop on all sides. Inside this fort the bare foundations of three or four beehive huts can be seen.

One of the better known stone forts is Cahermacneachtan, which translated means, the stone fort of the son of Neachtan. This is a circular fort of some one hundred feet in diameter. Foundations of rectangular buildings may be found within and there is a late medieval two-storeyed gateway. This fort was, in later times, the home of Ireland's most famous medieval law school, run by the O'Davorens. Duald Mac Firbis, the famous seventeenth century genealogist, studied here under Donald O'Davoren. Such was the extent of this complex in later centuries, it was described as 'O'Davoren's town' in 1657.

In contrast to the stone forts of the Burren is the massive hill fort at Moghane near Newmarket-on-Fergus. This dates from the Iron Age. A large cache of gold ornaments was discovered near it during the last century.

In addition to ring forts the development of a more sophisiticated habitat took place at this time — the crannóg. On islands in the many lakes, the Celts constructed villages of wood, mud and straw — fortresses as protection

Cahermacneachtan. A view of a small section of the perimeter wall.

against the wrath of the people they had dispossessed. If no island existed in a place which otherwise looked suitable, they used the limitless slave labour to construct an artificial one.

The crannóg was typically about one hundred feet in diameter with high stake walls to keep out the enemy. Normally, a crannóg contained three large round huts of straw roofs and wattled walls. An entire community settlement housed one family unit of about thirty people. Parents, children, uncles and aunts all lived and sometimes inter-married in the one crannóg village. Other than the permeable thatch roof and one small doorway, the huts were not well ventilated. With fires inside to provide light as well as for drying leather skins, the average age attained by primitive man was approximately half that of a present lifespan.

The crannóg was common in districts with lakes and marshes which made it safe from enemies. As well as having crannógs for dwellings our ancestors also built ringed forts on firm ground. The ring forts varied in diameter and had outer perimeters of earth and stones, and maybe walls of wooden stakes. Usually they were constructed on a hill or on high ground which afforded some natural protection. Traces of hundreds of such ringed forts can be seen throughout the county to this day. The forts contained, on average, three large huts with thatched roofs. A communal fire burned continuously out in the open and was used for cooking purposes. The only entrance, a wooden gate, was always closed at night. Animals from the outlying fields were often brought into the larger forts at night to be kept safe from enemies and preying wild beasts. Some forts contained souterrains, or undergound passages, possibly hiding places or food storage areas.

Today, there is a newly constructed crannóg and walled ringed fort (open to the public) at Craggaunowen near the village of Quin. These settlements did not originally exist at this location, but were recently constructed in the ancient fashion as typical examples.

The Celts were attracted to Ireland by the lure of gold. Try as they did, they found very little. It had all been traded by the Bronze Age people for Cornwall tin when it was accidently discovered at that time that tin alloyed with copper gave a greater degree of hardness to the metal, thus forming bronze. This development made tin a very necessary commodity in the making of bronze implements. County Wicklow was the main source of gold, but lumps of raw copper and small gold nuggets were occasionally picked off the ground. Some sources claim that gold was discovered in a number of the east Clare rivers.

Eventually, the Celtic masters took possession of all the tuaths, or local kingdoms. They then rented out the land to the previous owners at one third of its value per annum. The Celts were in complete control and during the early Iron Age the level of poverty was at its lowest since the Campignian colonisation at the beginning of the Stone Age. The climate improved slightly around 200 BC and conditions gradually improved for some time after that.

A great mingling of cultures undoubtedly took place. The menfolk spent most of their time hunting — a chase of the wild boar was much enjoyed. This

Reconstructed Crannóg at Craggaunowen.

left the women to cook and look after the family. It also allowed them to take care of all the possessions of the group, thus making them wise in bartering and in appreciating the value of goods. Consequently, in this type of society the woman occupied a place of considerable importance in the family grouping. The system is called matriarchal where the woman dominated the family line for positions of importance. Normally, men would take positions of leadership, but it was through the women that titles etc., were transferred. The son of the king's daughter was quite entitled to assume power when the line produced no other suitable heir.

Writing materials (except for stone) and the art of writing was not in existence at that time. Druids had symbols which they communicated to each other by using hand signals. The ogham writings, or characters, that we hear of today are those signs committed to stone. Their origin appears to have been Etruria, as they are very close to the early Greek alphabet of that period (circa 500 BC).

The ogham writing probably came into use in Ireland around AD 300. The name is derived from Ogmios, the Celtic god of writing. Its alphabet is made up of sets of five strokes on, diagonally across, or on either side of a central line — the central line could be the edge of a stone. Inscriptions began at the bottom and climbed to the top, continuing if necessary down the other side.

All knowledge deemed important to the tribes was therefore passed on in the vernacular, right up to the Christian era. This system is responsible for the many conflicting tales of what actually took place in a given incident. It has been discovered that some dates contradict each other, and similar occurrences have been attributed to different people.

The druids of the time were priests who enjoyed the respect of both ruler and ruled alike. They knew science and poetry, and had committed to memory long tracts of verse and folklore to be passed on to their students. Their religion demanded that a human sacrifice was required in time of war. In the first century AD, Strabo the historian, wrote of them: 'They used to stab a human being to death (one whom they devoted) in the back with a dagger and foretell the future from his convulsions.' They were, of course, very pagan and worshipped a supreme being who was represented to them in the sun, in fire and in sacrifice. As far as is known their important religious days were Samain — celebrated on 1 November: Imboly — celebrated on 1 February: Bealtaine — celebrated on 1 May: Lughnasa — celebrated on 1 August. Curiously, these same days are days of traditional customs right down to present times.

Ardsolus or Ath Solus, The Ford of Light, near Newmarket-on-Fergus, was the place of supreme worship in Clare shortly before the Christian era. Another district to derive its name from a place of worship is Tuamgraney, or Tuaim Greine, which means 'Altar of the Sun'. Many such names with 'greine' in their composition exist, indicating that the sun was a considerable influence on ancient people.

Savagery was common enough. Men were slain in many a petty squabble. Battles were organised for reasons which would seem avoidable to us under present-day circumstances. Cattle, land and slaves were sometimes fought over, with women taking their place in battle alongside the men.

A common intoxicating drink of the time was mead, a strong wine made from honey. Drunkenness was not unusual, although it was not regarded as being shameful. It was believed that the person in such a state was in communication with, and under the influence of, the gods.

As a result of the Celtic invasion, or Goidelic invasion as it is sometimes called, Ireland was divided into five-fifths. The five kingdoms were Ulster,

Munster, Connaught, Leinster and Midland (parts of present-day Leinster). At that time Connaught was the most powerful province with Clare attached to it. This national division took place around 50 BC.

The most renowned men of the Celtic invasion seem to have been the brothers Eber and Eremon. Many of the most important people of Ireland and Clare are said to descend from them. The tribes of Eremon are thought to have been more prominent in the northern half of the country, while the clans of Eber moved to the south, principally Munster. If this invader Eber did exist at all, as legend tells us he did, it would be from him that the prominent families of Clare can claim their inheritance.

In the second century AD, Conn of the Hundred Battles was generally regarded as being king of all Ireland. He was a descendant of Eremon, and his desire was to rule more than just his own half of the country. Conn had great difficulty in containing Mogha of the Silver Hand, who was king in Munster and was from the line of Eber. Mogha was very warlike, and is credited with defeating Conn in ten battles before he himself was slain in Moylea in the midlands by Conn's warriors.

However, the kingship of Munster had to be settled. Conn was most anxious that some amicable solution could be reached. He therefore gave his daughter, Sabia, in marriage to the only son and heir of Mogha, Oilioll Oluim. He further made him king of all Munster — the first king of that entire province. This tactic seemed to have worked quite well for we note that eight sons were born of the union. Oilioll Oluim willed that the descendants of his two sons, Eoghan Mor and Cormac Cas should alternate the crown of Munster between them. It is from Cormac Cas that the famous O'Briens of Clare are descended. This Cormac Cas married a daughter of Oisin, one of the most famous members of the Fianna. Oisin was a son of the legendary and most noble of all ancient Irish warriors, Fionn Mac Cumhaill. Also, a son-in-law of Conn, Conaire II, is the famed father of the three Carbris, one of whose descendants, Carbri Baiscin, populated Corca Baiscin in west Clare.

Fourth in descent from the marriage of Cormac Cas and the daughter of Oisin, was Luighaidh Meann. This man came to Clare to claim it for his own. Until that time, the county was one of the few places still strongly inhabited by the Firbolgs. In gradual skirmishes he drove the Firbolg before him, many of whom fled into Galway. Presumably, some of them remained entrenched in their remote huts and forts in the more inaccessible areas of the county. The vantage points along the river Fergus were not left to them. In strategic places like the delta meandering of the Fergus where Ennis now stands, they were ruthlessly killed or driven away.

It seems that the final gathering of the Firbolg took place in Galway. Here, they were completely overthrown in one last great battle at Moytura, near Cong. From Galway they fled the country, many of them sailed in crude boats to the Hebrides. Here they also found hostilities in store for them as they were driven out by the Picts.

Next, they returned to County Meath, during the reign of Cairbre Nia-Fear. This was shortly before the Christian era began in AD 432. Even though they made some agreements with the local chiefs, they were unable to form a lasting arrangement. So, one night they crossed the Shannon at Killaloe into the present county of Clare. The Firbolg were led by their chief, Umor, one of whose sons, Curta, settled in the now named Lough Cutra area just over the Clare border in County Galway. Another son led many of the Firbolg to the Burren where they remained. A third son, Aengus, made his way to the largest of the Aran Islands just off the Clare coast and stayed there. On one end of the island he built a large stone fort, which is well preserved to this day. He and his people lived there without further hindrance. The fort he built is since called Dun Aengus.

Luighaidh Meann, a Milesian of the Celtic race of people, had secured the area that is now Clare once and for all. This territory remained in possession of a member of his lineage down through the years. Also from him came the name Tuadh Mhumhann, or Thomond (North Munster) in English. The name was anglicised to the well-known Thomond version in later years by English administrations. This beginning by Luighaidh Meann was to be the start of a historic attachment to the same land by the same people down through the centuries to the present day. No other European people, save the Greeks and the Romans, can lay claim to such antiquity. Even though there would be many invasions suffered by the county, the intrinsic families managed to remain intact, remain Irish, and a race apart. They would still be in possession of the lands acquired by those ancient Celts right down to modern times.

Conal of the Fleet Steeds (his father was Luighaidh Meann), had a son called Cas — the man from whom all great Clare families can be traced. From his name is derived the title of Dalcassians for the Clare people who are descended from him.

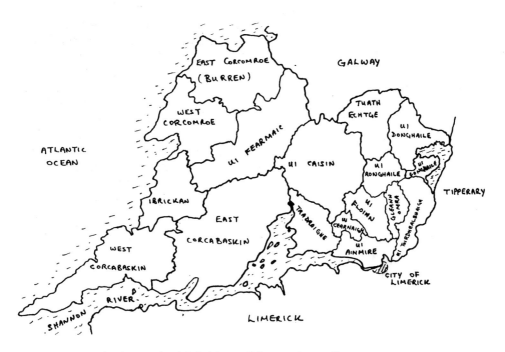

Ancient territorial divisions of Thomond, now County Clare.

The most renowned Dalcassian families which are traced from Cas are, amongst others: O'Briens, O'Deas, MacNamaras, MacMahons, O'Gradys, O'Mahoneys, MacClancys, MacInerneys, O'Quins, O'Hehirs and the O'Liddys.

The eldest son of Cas, who was named Blod, was the ancestor to the O'Briens. The O'Briens, who by right of birth as well as by force of their strong hand (lamh laidir), were most powerful in Clare. Second only to the O'Briens came the MacNamaras, who were descended from Caisin, second son of Cas.

Just before the introduction of Christianity in AD 432 social order had improved considerably in the country. Before the arrival of Patrick there had been twenty-seven high kings of Ireland at Tara, in County Meath. Public law and administration were respected. Ireland was one of the few countries in Europe at that time capable of enforcing law. It was also well advanced in culture and music. Story tellers and musicians were supplementing the druids as men of respect and were much sought after by chiefs and kings. The order of merit in the country at that time was as follows: the High King of Tara, subordinate kings and princes and their druids, petty chiefs, warriors, smiths, armourers, mechanics, and petty tillers of the soil.

In AD 365 Eighy Moyfeon, King of Ireland, died and was succeeded by Crimthan, King of Munster. Crimthan was head of the house of Eber and therefore a Dalcassian. The seat he vacated in Munster was first occupied by Corc of the race of Eoghan More, until AD 366. Corc was then succeeded by Conal Eachluaith, who was also a Dalcassian. The strength of the clan can be seen from the fact that two of their numbers were ruling Munster and Ireland at the same time.

Crimthan's sister was extremely bitter about the appointment as she wanted her own son Brian to take over. To dispose of Crimthan she prepared a poisoned drink, which she sipped first. This act was to ensure that Crimthan would not become suspicious. Crimthan died in AD 379 near Cratloe, on a mountain called Slieve-Oighe-an-Righ (the hill of the king's death), after the incident. Ironically, the kingship fell to Niall who was a son of the old king's second wife. But with the death of Crimthan the connection between the Dalcassians and the high kingship ceased for another six hundred years.

At this period the Irish high kings were notorious for their military expeditions to Britain and Gaul. They frequently plundered the coastal settlements and returned with many slaves to be sold to Irish lords. Niall of the Nine Hostages brought back a horde of young captives around AD 405, one of whom was to change the course of Irish history. The slave's name was Patrick. His teaching would send men, not on military expeditions for human bodies, but on missions of peace in the name of Christianity, back to the land that they had previously plundered.

Chapter 3

Christianity and the Norsemen (432 ⸗ AD 1014)

Patrick was detained as a slave herding sheep on the slopes of Slieve Mish, in County Antrim. After six long years in captivity he managed to escape by boarding a vessel sailing from Wicklow for the Continent. In France he studied for the priesthood, and when he decided to return on a mission to Ireland to convert the heathens who had enslaved him, he was consecrated a bishop. In AD 432 he landed on the east coast of the country and immediately proceeded to the high king of Tara. He sought permission from King Laoghaire to preach Christianity to his subjects. The King consented but did not take up the new religion himself. All the Irish kings were reluctant to turn away from the influence of their druids. Indeed, there was not a Christian king in Cashel until AD 490.

The impoverished classes embraced the new religion with considerable zeal because it offered hope and a form of salvation for them. Most opposition to Patrick and to his Christian teaching came from the powerful druids, who were quick to realise that their positions of authority were in jeopardy. The pagan beliefs and superstitious ways of the people were not entirely demolished, but allowed to blend with the new religion. Superstition and fairy beliefs are still widespread amongst the Irish down to modern times.

Some religious celebration days which have transcended from ancient times right down to the present day include St. Brigid's Day, celebrated on 1 February each year. In olden days it was the feast of Imboly, or a new Fertility Feast. The Celtic Samhan was observed on 1 November as a barrier to superstition, now known as All Saints Day. Halloween reaches back to our pre-Christian ancestors; for them it was the turning of the year, a time when the spirits of the other world attempted to escape back into this world.

During this period when Patrick and his followers set out to establish their church there were no towns or villages in the country. The Roman Empire, which had played a major role in the development of infrastructures like roads, towns and central administration, never reached Ireland. So, a monastic church was developed to suit the local conditions. It involved the building of monasteries in isolated areas. These housed the religious monks who would travel out from their monastic bases to preach and administer the new religion.

Patrick travelled much of Ireland preaching the new faith and establishing churches. Many bishops were appointed during his circuit and invariably, the candidates were local chiefs of some authority.

Although he came as far as Patrick's Well in Limerick, Patrick never crossed the Shannon into the present county of Clare. From an elevated position he could see most of the county and is reputed to have blessed the kingdom. He is further credited with stating that a native son of Clare would grow up who would administer the new religion to its people. About forty years later a man came from Moghlacha, three miles outside Kilrush, and became one of Clare's most renowned holy men. In AD 488 St Senan was born and having spent some time in religious work outside the county he returned to establish many churches around his native area.

He had monasteries built in Inislunga and on Inisluaidhe, at the junction of the Fergus and Shannon estuaries. Also constructed under his guidance was a house of holy retreat on Mutton Island. But the place most associated with St Senan would be Inis Cathaigh (Scattery Island) where a church and round tower were constructed. He lived there from AD 540 to 560 and was buried on the island when he died. The monastery was ravaged by the Vikings in 816 and again in 835, and may even have been occupied by them for a time until Brian Boru routed them. Additions were made to the settlement in the thirteenth and fourteenth centuries. In 1359 Pope Innocent VI at Avignon appointed a bishop to the island, but he was not recognised by the local clergy. It is still a place of pilgrimage today and St Senan's bed of stone in the monastery is presumed to be the resting place of the saint. Curiously, he allowed no women on the island during his lifetime.

Another monastic church of note is the one currently in use (the oldest in the country) at Tuamgraney. A monastic settlement was founded on the site in AD 550. The western portion of the church is reputed to have been rebuilt by the abbot, Cormac O Killeen in 969. Even Brian Boru carried out some repair work on it circa AD 1000.

Except for some local kings, and isolated districts, the majority of the population had become Christian in the span of one hundred years. Monasteries were founded and soon became seats of learning for literary, scientific and religious disciplines. Foreign students attended from all over Europe, and lived simple lives of austerity in the monasteries with their tutors. From those great centres of religious zeal, missionaries went to all parts of Europe. They were enthused with a burning desire to impart their new-found faith to the unbelieving of Britain, France, Germany, Italy and Switzerland.

Perhaps it is given very little attention, and is possibly overshadowed by the religion itself, but certainly just as important to the cultural development of the country was the introduction of the art of writing. For ever since the skill came into common use, some records of events were kept. History prior to the introduction of Christianity is all based on the vernacular, and as such is subject to much doubt.

At Killaloe, St Flannan had a little chapel, or oratory, situated close to the Shannon. Killaloe at that time was the hub of more activity than was the present Ennis area. There were churches at Corrovorrin and Drumcliffe prior to the O'Briens founding a monastery in the thirteenth century at the place where Ennis now stands. It is from Killaloe that the diocese in the Dalcassian district of Clare and North Tipperary derived its present family name. Kil-

Ornamental Romanesque doorway of Dysert-O'Dea church.
Church at this site from the eighth century, founded by St. Tola.

laloe was the seat of the first bishop and/or abbots who ruled the district.

Not much is known of the exact time of St Flannan's life. It is recorded sketchily, that a St Flannan did exist in the middle of the eighth century. His strong influence in the church of Killaloe is due to the fact that he was a sixth generation ancestor of Brian Boru. This relationship greatly pleased the famous king. Brian did his utmost to sustain the memory of the holy man in his family. Subsequently, churches built by the Dalcassians were dedicated to Flannan. The present high-pitched Gothic church in Killaloe was completed in its present state by the Dalcassians in the thirteenth century.

Other than churches and monasteries, the normal habitation of the people was still very crude. Standards of living remained very low amongst the vast majority, which gave rise to many unsanitary conditions. There is a report of yellow plague in the country in AD 666, one of the most frightening diseases to ravage any land. Amongst its victims at that time was Diarmait, High King of Ireland. There were numerous unrecorded deaths, and it would be foolhardy to estimate numbers.

Partial round tower and ruined church at Drumcliffe cemetery, near Ennis. Dates from the thirteenth century. Rebuilt in the fifteenth century.

After AD 700 it is recorded that a bishop was equal in standing and privileges to the king of a tuath. The lowest ruling rank of Aire Desa was required to possess fourteen cumals (1 cumal equalled 34 acres) and a grinding mill, a kiln to dry grain, and a barn to store his corn in. A person not being noble by birth needed double the property of his counter-part in nobility in order to equal him in dignity. He was obliged to keep an open house for all visitors and could refuse no man hospitality, no matter how many times he called — perhaps an explanation of the present-day famous Irish hospitality.

The skilled people were inferior to the nobility, but were privileged freemen. Belonging to this class were the carpenters, masons, goldsmiths, coppersmiths and blacksmiths. Those skilled in arts and crafts, such as physicians and lawyers, were also classified in this category. Education in itself was seen as an entitlement to be a freeman. The lawyers referred to above only served in the lower courts and were of modest standing. Of the musicians, only harpers were regarded as being noble. Other musicians, public entertainers and minor craftsmen, had no affiliations or positions of privilege. The above qualified people could be generally regarded as commoners of good standing.

Below the commoners or skilled people came two classes of vassals. The first type were nobles of an inferior grade who were entitled to receive livestock from the local king. In return they provided him with an annual gratuity and military service when required. A second type of vassal had less rights but had greater obligations of payment for stock taken over from their supporters. Normally their rent consisted of various types of food given to their king when he visited them twice a year.

A look at the dress of the early Irish shows the uniqueness of these island people as a separate race. Up to the invasion of the Milesians the inhabitants wore animal skins. Thereafter, a gradual change to a more sophisticated dress form took place. The garments they later wore were distinctive from those of other peoples.

The Truis or Straith Bracca was a lower body garment of various colours. It covered the ankles, legs and thighs and fitted high on the loins, so close that the movement of every muscle was clearly displayed.

The Cota was a kind of thin woollen skirt, made of wool and plaited with strips of linen dyed yellow and attached to it. It was a long garment which could be wrapped round the body and made fast by a girdle folded round the loins. On some styles the sleeves were quite short while others showed a preference for sleeves which came right down to the waist.

A Cochal, or the upper garment, was something like a long cloak with a large hanging collar or hood. It came in many different colours and reached as low as the middle of the thighs. The Cochal was fringed with a border of shagged hair. Because it was slung over the shoulder it was fastened on the breast with a clasp or buckle.

Another item of clothing of the developing Irish dress was the Cannabhas. It was large and loose, indeed not unlike the Cochal and was probably worn as a substitute for it. The Cannabhas covered the shoulders and spread over the whole body. When the hood of the Cannabhas was drawn over the head it served to completely disguise the wearer.

On the head it was usual to wear the Barrad, a conical cap. This was not unlike the cap later worn by the grenadiers. It had one distinct difference, the cone of the Barrad was left to hang loosely behind.

Let us not pass without mentioning the dress of the druids. This, we are told, was uniformally and universally white, being emblematic of the purity of their minds. In order to render their appearance more venerable they allowed their beards to grow to great lengths, flowing onto their breasts.

There were three classes of labourers working on the lord's estates who were without political rights of any kind. These people were the original inhabitants of the region before the Celts arrived. They were systematically pushed to the bottom of the pile by the new and more sophisticated invader. They were allowed to settle on the land and were hired as workers to perform menial tasks. The worst off of this class of people were the mug (a male slave), and the cumal (a female slave). Their position of slavery was one which the new religion was to fight consistently. It is not surprising to find therefore, that the number of slaves in the country diminished quite considerably in the early Christian era. However, the lowly practice of trafficking in human beings was to be reintroduced later on when the Norsemen came on the scene.

It is said that the King of Cashel (a Munster king) was entitled to receive from the territory of Corcobaskin the following:— a thousand oxen and a thousand cows. He could also claim from the territory of the Burren, one thousand cows, one thousand oxen, one thousand rams and a thousand cloaks. These figures would appear to be somewhat exaggerated but it can be taken that considerable property was delivered to the kings each year in tributes. The landowner would do his utmost to remain in favour with his king. There was always the danger of a petty king being replaced, if gifts to his over-lord were not quite up to scratch. It was not all one way traffic, as the king had certain commitments to the rulers who served under him. For instance, we note that the king of Corcobaskin was entitled to receive a drinking horn, two steeds and a king's apparel each year from the king at Cashel.

The Munster kings at that time relied heavily on the loyalty of the Dalcassians who always supplied them with an army in time of battle. Such was their willingness to fight for the king that the following was attributed to them:— 'The Dalcassians were the first into battle and the last out of it'. The Thomond clans were usually out-voted in the provincial election of kings, and for that reason only many more of the Eoghanachts became Munster kings. Thomond, for a while, fell from prominence due to the strength of the south Munster kingdom. Commencing about the middle of the eighth century, Cashel was ruled by a race of Eoghanacht priest-kings. One of them, Cormac MacCullenan, was a great scholar and a man of remarkable character.

The ninth century opened on a disastrous note for the county. In AD 801, on the eve of St Patrick's day, a great storm howled along the west coast, with much thunder, lightning and raging seas. The land between Baltard and Hag's Head collapsed and plunged into the sea. The earthquake occurred near some villages, and took with it many hundreds of inhabitants. Reports of the time suggested that a thousand souls were lost. With the collapsing rock and earth the coastline became much more dangerous. An island just off the mainland was split into three fragments and the entire area was left devastated by the forces of nature.

The battle against nature was indeed hard at times but never as consistently tyrannical as the foe who was at that time making serious inroads into the country. Once again the highly navigable rivers provided the springboard for this latest invasion. The Norsemen, who were until then quite busy raiding most of Europe, turned their attentions to Ireland. In the kingdom of Thomond it is likely that they first sailed their long galleys into the wide mouth of the river Shannon. It was quite possible for them to travel right up to Lough Derg and even further upstream — into the heart of the land.

The inhabitants of the country were taken completely by surprise. They were not organised to resist this new threat and it took them some time to come to grips with the problem. With fine armour and axes and long swords, the Norsemen raided the many monasteries which contained precious objects of valuable metals. The lush grazing lands were an open invitation to those hardy invaders. They slaughtered cattle when required, and some hostages were carried off. This was a practice which was later taken up by the native princes. Feidhlim, a son of Crimthan, king of Munster in 831 and 832, burned and sacked the monastic settlement at Clonmacnoise itself.

Flann, monarch of Ireland, was appalled at these outrages. In 877 he marched on Munster and attacked the kingdom from Killaloe to Cork. The then king at Cashel, Cormac, retaliated by rounding up his own clans, which included the Eoghanachts and the Dalcassians, who between them inflicted a heavy defeat on the old enemy. Seemingly, for this service, Cormac declared Lorcan a prince of the Dalcassians. It was further confirmed to him that he was in direct line with their common ancestor Oilioll Oluim.

Early in the tenth century, the Norse became more entrenched in the country because they had set up strong fortresses in Dublin, Wexford, Waterford and Cork. When they finally occupied Limerick in AD 920, they had completed a chain of Viking colonies and harbour fortresses which fairly held the country in a vice-like grip.

In the middle of the tenth century the Dalcassians were ruled by a man called Cennédig (Kennedy). This chief was descended from the royal line of Oilioll Oluim, who was father to both Eoghan Mór (of the Eoghanachts) and Cormac Cas (of the Dalcassians). Cennédig had two sons, Mahon (the oldest), and Brian who was born in Thomond in either AD 940 or AD 941. Some sources put his birthdate at 926 AD, which would make him an incredible eighty-eight year old at the battle of Clontarf. Between them they spearheaded a great campaign against the Norsemen. As will be seen later Brian was to receive unusually sterling support from a deposed high king, namely Malachy of Meath. Malachy had attained the high kingship by defeating the Norse army at Tara, Co. Meath, in AD 980.

By and large the invaders had most of the country subdued except for some resistance by Malachy in Meath and Brian in Thomond. Malachy scored a few noteworthy victories over the Norse, but he lacked collective support from the rest of the country. In Thomond the Dalcassians were a real thorn in the side of the Norse (mostly Danes) who were commanded by Ivor in Limerick. The best they could hope for was to contain the non-stop-fighting Dalcassians within the present county of Clare. With the Shannon affording them a natural boundary which was not easily penetrable, the Norse felt that this was their best tactic. But Brian fought a continuous guerrilla action. From the woods and hills of Clare he made frequent forays into Limerick. However, he had difficulty at times in keeping a fighting force in the field. It was reported that at one stage in his campaign that he was down to fifteen men.

Such was the fame of the brothers Mahon and Brian, that in 963 on the death of Donnchad, Mahon felt he could justifiably lay claim to the throne of Cashel. In order to consolidate his position he felt it necessary to crush the Norse of Limerick, because Ivor and his followers were allied to the Eoghanachts. The forces met at Sulcoit near Tipperary town. The result was a raging hand-to-hand battle which lasted from sunrise to mid-day. The Norse under Ivor were forced to retreat in haste to Limerick. However, many were captured and killed without mercy, and the rest were put into slavery. The date of this notable victory for the Dalcassians is recorded at AD 968 in *The Annals of the Four Masters.*

Ivor, together with his two Eoghanacht allies, Donovan and Molloy, managed to escape overseas. Mahon ruled as king of Munster, spending much of his reign at war with the Danes.

After a suitable absence Ivor returned to conspire once again with Donovan and Molloy. Mahon was enticed, on some pretext or another, into Molloy's country in the heart of Munster. While there he was treacherously murdered on the Cork/Limerick border. This foul act, as well as enraging Brian, made it possible for him to take over the seat at Cashel. The great leader soon made it plain that it was a foolish man indeed who would provoke him. He immediately set about revenging the dastardly murder of his brother. As we shall see, blood flowed freely throughout the land until he had gained his satisfaction.

Brian routed the Norse out of the islands in the Shannon estuary and drove some more from the territory of Corcobaskin, in south-west Clare, in AD 975. He then went into Limerick and slew Ivor, an old protagonist, on Coney Island in 977. While he was there he also attacked and killed Donovan who had conspired in the death of his brother. Another of the chief conspirators in the murder of Mahon was Maelmuidh. This man was also attacked and beaten by the Dalcassians under Brian. Brian's own son, Morogh, who could only have been a teenager at the time, had the honour of slaying Maelmuidh of the Eoghanachts (Eugenians). The victorious Dalcassians returned to Thomond laden with the spoils of war. Because they had been firmly installed in the Munster seat, there was much rejoicing at the palace in Kincora. It was a great source of satisfaction to the Dalcassians that they had reinstated a Thomond clan member to the Munster kingship once again. All along they had been unjustly deprived of that right due entirely to the greater strength of clan members of the southern Eoghanachts. For many years prior to this event the Eoghanachts had consistently refused to employ the alternate change of rule plan, as laid down by Brehon law.

After this Brian turned his attention to Ireland as a whole. First, he over-ran Ossary. Malachy, the king there, made retaliatory incursions into Thomond itself. He attacked Magh Adhair (the inauguration place of the Dalcassian chiefs). At that time the site was marked by a great oak tree situated half way between Quin and Tulla. As a point of interest, the inauguration ceremony consisted of the Wand of Power being handed over by the second most powerful clan in Thomond, the MacNamaras. After the attack on Magh Adhair Brian launched a scathing attack into the land of the High King — West Meath.

Thereafter, peace reigned for a time, except for one raid by the Dalcassians (not led by Brian) into Connaught in AD 987. During this particular sortie they suffered a heavy defeat at the hands of the powerful Connaught clans.

Brian devoted much of his time to restoring the old Celtic values. He built, or rebuilt, many churches including some at Killaloe, Iniscaltra and Tuamgraney. Monasteries were restored and old seats of learning were revived. Books, which had been destroyed or lost, were sent for to foreign lands. With the establishment of the seaports by the Norse, commercial enterprise with overseas settlements developed and increased. In some instances the Norse were incorporated into the Gaelic way of life and Brian himself ruled that those in his kingdom should serve him in time of warfare. He also constructed roads and built bridges as well as fortifying his own palace at Kincora.

The only medieval convent for nuns in the diocese of Killaloe, Killone Abbey. Founded by Donal More O'Brien, King of Thomond in the twelfth century. Located near the isolated Newhall Lake, three miles from Ennis.

By 993 Brian was in a position to command his Norse allies to sail their long galleys up the Shannon to Lough Ree, from where he was able to dominate Connaught and Meath. He had learned a valuable tactic from his old Norse enemies — warfare from the waterways. In 995 we find Brian waging war deep into Malachy's territory of West Meath. This constituted an attack on the high kingship itself, but Malachy being the great leader that he was, settled with Brian to divide the country between them. It was agreed in 998 that Malachy should rule the northern half with Brian as supreme king of the southern half, along with the vassalages of Dublin and the Norse towns.

In Leinster all things were not going well either. Sitric and Maelmora, the Norse and Leinster allies, were making attempts to recover the kingdom of Leinster. To immediately quell the unrest, Brian marched from Kincora to engage and defeat the Norse and Leinster allies at Glenmama, west of Dublin, in AD 999. At that time Brian was about fifty-nine years of age and he had been gradually handing over much control to his two sons, Morogh and Taigh. However, he was not beyond falling for a cleverly devious woman named Gormflath, who was previously married to Malachy. She was also responsible for prompting Sitric and Maelmora to rebel against Brian. He married her and she bore him a son called Donnchad. Due entirely to her influence he restored Sitric to his old command of Dublin, and gave to Maelmora the kingship of

Clare Abbey — Abbey of the Canons regular of St. Augustine. Founded by Donal More O'Brien, King of Thomond, shortly before he died in 1194. Located near Clarecastle.

Leinster.

Brian was still aching for the supreme kingship of Ireland, and with that end in mind he engaged Malachy at Tara. Supporting him were all of the Munster and many of the Leinster clans, with some of the Norse warriors and chieftains who lived under his rule. Malachy called on the Uí Neill from the north to support him. They failed to respond to his call and this forced him to concede Brian's claim for the high kingship without actually doing battle with him. The year of Brian's accession was 1002. Since the death of Crimthan, about six hundred years before, no Dalcassian chief had been high king. When Brian took over he carried out the circuit of the High King with a pomp and splendour never seen before or after. From Kincora he marched through Connaught and up to Armagh in Ulster. Having attended mass in the church at Armagh he laid twenty ounces of gold as a gift on the altar. From Armagh he marched to Tara, on to Dublin, back through Leinster and Ossory, and finally to the Munster seat at Cashel.

This was the most emphatic and triumphant claim over the whole Gaelic race by any high king. The good work of rebuilding which he had started in the kingdom of Munster, he then expanded to all of the country. In 1007 he revived the great Fair of Tailtean, an event which had not been celebrated for eighty years previously. Brian's great Celtic revival signalled an end to the Norse tyranny. Every corner of Ireland acknowledged him as supreme ruler. Such was his authority that he was able to claim tributes from all kingdoms. Because he was so able to claim such previously unknown quantities of tributes he became known as Brian Boru (Brian of the Tributes).

He was entitled to hundreds of cows, hogs, cloaks and mantles from Connaught, Tirconnel, Tirowen and Leinster. The Norse of Dublin were equally obliged to fulfil their obligations to him. It was a fact that he annually received 365 pipes of red wine from the Danes in Limerick. Brian had ten years as high king in which to build up the country to a new level of sophistication. He succeeded admirably in this great task. Once again Brian Boru established the Christian Church with its principal seat of rule in Armagh.

Gormflath, the woman cast aside by both Brian and Malachy, was again stirring up rebellion in the hearts of Sitric and Maelmora in the province of Leinster. Malachy was finding it difficult enough to keep order in the northern half of the country. He was obliged to summon Brian to his aid in 1013. Brian besieged Dublin from September until Christmas of that year, eventually being forced to retire due to lack of provisions.

Early in the year 1014 more unrest followed in the east of the country. Gathering up all his Dalcassians, the Munster and south Connaught clans, he once again marched on Dublin. On this occasion he was resolved to squash forever every last usurper, in particular the Norse who were at the root of every insurrection. His army arrived on the high ground between Dublin and the Tolka with the opposing forces sighting each other on the day before Good Friday. Malachy was also standing by with a contingent of his own troops and bands of Celts were simultaneously arriving from Scotland to assist them. Brian was about seventy-four years of age at that time and was therefore too old for the strenuous hand-to-hand fighting. His son Morogh and grandson Turloch led the Dalcassians to battle.

Facing them were two thousand of the best fighting men the Norse could muster from Ireland, Scotland and the Isle of Man. They were further assisted by the Leinster clans of O'Byrnes and O'Tooles, fierce fighting men all. Brian relied mainly on his vastly experienced and trustworthy Dalcassians whom he pushed to the front of the lines.

As the sun rose over Clontarf on Good Friday morning of 23 April 1014, the forces attacked each other in a confrontation that was to last until sunset. With relentless close quarter fighting, where the axe and the sword were the favoured weapons, it was no place for the untried. The bow and arrow was not a weapon of the time so it meant that all killing was done at close range. Strength, aggressiveness and alertness were attributes which stood the Dalcassians in good stead on that fateful day at Clontarf.

Brian prayed for victory and remained in his tent between the lines. Morogh led the Dalcassians and towards evening he broke the Norse lines and killed their leader Sigurd on the field. Sitric took no part but watched the battle from the safety of the castle ramparts. When Maelmora fell, the allies were routed and Brian's forces came in hot pursuit. Morogh, the hero of the day, whose hand became locked to his sword in a death grip after twelve hours of continuous fighting, was killed while attempting to adjust his grip in order to stab an enemy laying on the ground.

The retreating Norse made for their weir on the Tolka so that they might get to their ships at Clontarf. But the tide was in and created a flood so that many of them were drowned while trying to escape. Morogh's son, Turloch, was also drowned as he pursued them. One of the fleeing Norsemen, Brodar, seeing Brian unguarded in his tent, slew the defenceless king. A number of the king's bodyguards gave chase and caught up with Brodar. He was savagely killed and disembowelled.

The Norse tyranny had been utterly destroyed at Clontarf by Brian. His forces were unable to take Dublin itself and shortly returned to Kincora under the command of another son, Taigh.

Brian's body was brought to Armagh, where the clergy buried it beside the high altar with the utmost honour and dignity. So ended the greatest reign of any Celtic monarch. The proud Dalcassian king had restored culture, order and religion to a land shattered by the ruthless invader.

During his reign Brian had encouraged the adoption of surnames which gave us the now world famous family names like O'Brien (O'Brian), O'Connor, MacNamara and many more. Brian left a noble heritage, which, if it had continued and been built on, would have made the country truly a strong nation. Unfortunately, leaders of his quality were a rarity and the period which followed his death was like a step back into the past.

The following poem (attributed to MacLiag, 1015) translated from the Irish by James Clarence Mangan (1803-1849) is indicative of the eminence of Brian and his kingdom centred at Kincora.

KINCORA

Oh, where, Kincora! is Brian the Great?
And where is the beauty that once was thine?
Oh, where are the princes and nobles that sate
At the feast in thy halls, and drank the red wine?
  Where, oh, Kincora?

Oh, where, Kincora! are thy valorous lords?
Oh, wither, thou hospitable! are they gone?
Oh, where are the Dalcassians of the Golden Swords?
And where are the warriors Brian led on?
  Where, oh, Kincora?

And where is Murrough, the descendant of kings
The defeater of a hundred — the daringly brave —
Who set but slight store by jewels and rings —
Who swam down the torrent and laughed at its waves?
  Where, oh, Kincora?

And where is Donogh, King Brian's worthy son?
And where is Conaing, the beautiful chief?
And Kian, and Corc? Alas! they are gone —
They have left me this night alone with my grief,
  Left me, Kincora!

And where are the chiefs with whom Brian went forth,
The ne'er vanquished sons of Erin the Brave,
The great king ot Onaght, renowned for his worth,
And the hosts of Baskinn, from the western wave?
  Where, oh, Kincora?

And where is that youth of majestic height,
The faith-keeping prince of the Scots? — Even he,
As wide as his fame was, as great as his might,
Was tributary, oh, Kincora, to thee!
        Thee, oh, Kincora!

They are gone, those heroes of royal birth,
Who plundered no churches, and broke no trust,
'Tis weary for me to be living on earth
While they, oh, Kincora, lie low in the dust!
        Low, oh, Kincora!

Oh, never again will princes appear,
To rival the Dalcassians of Cleaving Swords!
I can never dream of meeting afar or anear,
In the east or the west, such heroes and lords!
        Never, Kincora!

Oh, dear are the images my memory calls up
Of Brian Boru! — how he would never miss
To give me at the banquet the first bright cup!
Oh, why did he heap on me honour like this?
        Why, oh, Kincora?

I am MacLiag, and my home is on the lake;
Thither often, to that palace whose beauty is fled
Came Brian to ask me, and I went for his sake.
Oh, my grief! that I should live, and Brian be dead!
        Dead, oh, Kincora?

Original coat of arms of the O'Briens.

King Brian Boroimhe killed by the Viking at Clontarf, 1014.
(Reproduced from Cusack's History of the Irish Nation)

Chapter 4

Dalcassians at War
(1014 — 1168)

With the death of Brian the high kingship slipped from the Dalcassians back to Malachy of Leinster. The clan was further weakened by the loss of a son and a grandson at Clontarf. Even as the survivors of Brian's army were returning to Kincora after the battle of Clontarf they encountered more hostilities. These assaults, from Irish clans, were unbefitting any army which had just rid the country of one of its worst menaces. While marching through Ossory, MacGiolla Phádraig attacked them in overpowering numbers. Undaunted, the Dalcassians fixed stakes into the ground to which they tied their wounded for support. An able bodied soldier was posted by each one for protection. This act of determination so gripped the attackers that they withdrew with an even greater respect for the Thomond men.

On returning to Kincora, there was some dissension between the brothers Taigh and Donogh as to who should sit on the throne of Munster. The clans for the most part favoured Taigh for kingship, but he was still required to overcome a claim from the southern Eoghanachts who disputed every decision vigorously.

Taigh and Donogh defeated Donal of the Eoghanachts in a decisive battle at Limerick. By so doing they had established their claim to the Munster throne. In 1014 the clans of Connaught saw their opportunity to strike at the weakened Dalcassians. The palace at Kincora was subsequently raided and destroyed. However, the men of Thomond were able to muster a raiding party to go as far north as Lough Ree, and return with some plunder. Things remained reasonably quiet for a while, but the brothers Taigh and Donogh continued to argue as to which of them should be king.

When Malachy of Leinster died in 1028, Donogh made his move towards the high office. Because his brother Taigh stood in his way he connived with the people of Ely O'Carrol against him. They succeeded in murdering Taigh rather shamefully. Donogh then gathered under his banner those who served his father, Brian, and marched through Meath and on to Dublin. He returned through Leinster and Ossory where he took many captives. He attacked and subdued all who did not give him immediate recognition. This action gave him some measure of respect. The sovereignty of the southern half (Leath Mogha) of the country was grudgingly given to him.

Donogh occupied himself with much hostilities about Ireland until he was generally recognised as High King in 1049. However, the general state of the country was deplorable in the extreme. With fighting and bustling for positions, with a lack of co-operation and treachery rife, it was no surprise to find living conditions at a low level. Crops and husbandry could not have received the attention they deserved. To make matters worse the climate of the time was extremely harsh and destroyed many of the crops. Fruit, fish and milk were hard to come by, so the people turned to stealing and plunder. Things were so bad that Donogh, at a Killaloe conference, had to enforce special laws of order in an effort to preserve some level of stability.

From his own example it can be said that Donogh was more of a law breaker than anyone else. He raided the territory of Diarmuid, king of Leinster. His action was quickly repaid by the Leinster king who attacked Thomond from end to end. Such was the thoroughness of the raid that the fortress of Dun-tri-Liag near Corbally in Limerick was knocked to the ground. The structure had been originally built by Cormac Cas and enlarged and fortified by Brian Boru.

While Donogh was down in South Munster, his home territory was attacked again. On this occasion it was Aedh O'Connor who carried away great spoils from Tradaree and Corcobaskin in south Clare. Hostilities had become an every day occurrence in the kingdom.

In an effort to demonstrate contempt for his enemies, Donogh sent his son Morogh of the Short Shield, to the northern part of the country to chastise his enemies there. However, Turlogh in the north, who was an ally of Aedh O'Connor gave him more than he had bargained for. Fifteen of Morogh's chief's were killed and four hundred more of his men were left dead on the battlefield.

Donogh was also to learn that staying within his own boundaries of Thomond was not enough to win some peace from Aedh O'Connor. He sent a raiding party into Thomond within a year. The fortress of the king at Kincora, as well as the village of Killaloe, were plundered and destroyed. His final great defeat came in a fierce battle near Tipperary where he lost many of his best fighting men. The Leinster king then installed his own fosterson, Turlogh (who was also Donogh's son-in-law), as king of Thomond. This arrangement seemed to satisfy all concerned — relative peace reigned for some years in the kingdom. Certainly, Donogh had displeased many people, and he appears to have been a man of little virtue. To cleanse his soul of his foul deeds he later travelled to the Holy See in Rome where he spent the rest of his years doing penance for his sins.

The above mentioned Turlogh O'Brien received another lucky break towards his career advancement when two powerful Irish princes, Diarmuid King of Leinster and Aedh O'Connor of Connaught, were slain in battle. There were no other serious contenders for the throne in the south and he needed only one other kingdom to support him. When this required support did not come willingly he gathered up a great army of Munster men and other allies. In 1075 he marched on the north of the country. Once there he demanded hostages as tokens of submission. Instead of submission he met with violent opposition. He was subsequently defeated in a hard-fought battle in County Louth. However, he was more successful in the province of Connaught where he formed an alliance with the king, Rory O'Connor. He was now loosely recognised as High King of all Ireland, even it under stern opposition from the north of the country. Such was the uncertainty of his position he was obliged to keep up his attacks on those who disputed his claim. For example, we note that in 1080 he was in the field again, sacking Dublin.

By 1084 the people of West Thomond were assailed once more by the Connaught tribes. They looted and burned around the districts of Tuamgraney, Moynoe and Killaloe, which were areas of considerable importance at that time. Turlogh and his Dalcassian warriors were busy fighting in County Meath when the blitz took place. Of course this incident did not pass unpunished by Turlogh, who shortly afterwards plundered the Kingdom of Leitrim (Muinter Eolais). Turlogh was at that time well advanced in years and it was probably his last great campaign. He died peacefully at the palace of Kincora in AD 1086. He was in his seventieth year when he succumbed which was considered advanced for the time

A son of Turlogh, Murtagh More O'Brien, next took over the Dalcassian and Munster kingships. Murtagh was duly installed by the MacNamaras at the royal rath of Magh Adhair in AD 1086. As was the accepted way of life, he immediately made raids outside of Thomond. He scored a number of small successes in the kingdom of Leinster.

Next we find him attacking Connaught by the novel method of using boats on the Shannon and on the sea. Rory O'Connor defeated him and captured many of his vessels. Murtagh was taken prisoner and detained for a time.

Donal MacLaughlin O'Neill, King of Ireland, and Rory O'Connor teamed up and spent considerable time and energy plundering the Kingdom of Thomond. They raided and looted as far south as Emly and Bruree, both of which are situated in the present county of Limerick. On their return they ransacked the palace of Kincora, capturing many Dalcassian princes and some of their Danish allies. Further incursions by the Dalcassians into Connaught proved futile, and only resulted in more plundering of East Thomond (Tipperary North) by the Connaught men.

Murtagh was a warlike individual and there are many more accounts of his hostilities about the country. An example of the callousness of his character can be seen from the fact that he delivered a chief, MacCoirten, whom he had captured on a northern raid, to his most bitter enemies — the O'Learys. It will be remembered that the deliverance of hostages over to their enemies meant a fate worse than death. In this instance Murtagh received eight other hostages in return, one hundred cows and thirty ounces of gold.

His burning ambition was to achieve the kingship of all-Ireland. After indifferent successes, Murtagh finally won a notable victory in the north. This proved to be enough to give him a favourable majority of support. Like his grandfather, Brian Boru, he immediately set out on a victorious circuit round the country. He was received everywhere without resistance. There was great rejoicing when he and his army returned in triumph to Kincora.

In 1114 Murtagh was laid low by a bout of sickness. His brother Dermot took advantage of the situation and immediately assumed control without being asked to do so. When Murtagh recovered his health he quickly deposed Dermot and resumed his position of power in the kingdom. In 1116 there was another direct attack on the royal palace at Kincora, again by the Connaught men. The fortress which had been erected by Brian Boru, was destroyed and much booty seized. Dermot died shortly afterwards in the year 1118. A year later Murtagh died and he was buried in the church of his ancestors in Killaloe.

A son of Dermot's named Donogh, was later installed as bishop of Killaloe. At that time bishops were usually selected from the noble or ruling class. An appointment to the position was as much political as it was religious.

Murtagh's two sons were next to take over the positions of power. Conor-na-Catharach was made king of Munster and his brother Turlogh assumed the kingship of Thomond. As was the family tradition, and indeed a necessity for success, Conor waged war in Leinster in order to assert his position. He managed to subdue the Danes in their settlements of Waterford and Dublin.

By now the Connaught kings were really thriving on the diversions of the Munster clans. Once again they captured Killaloe in 1119, and in 1124 they went over the falls of Doonass in their boats to plunder along the banks of the lower Shannon. They sailed as far as the island of Foynes and returned home safely.

Thinking that there was something to be gained from these naval excursions, Conor tried his hand at attacking Connaught by sailing up the Shannon from Kincora. His fleet was still in Lough Derg when he encountered the Connaughtmen's vessels. Both forces obliged us with the unusual spectacle of a naval battle on the Shannon. Long boats were used, powered by a mainsail and long banks of oars. No doubt the expertise came from the Danes who were dispersed about the country and had affiliations to numerous local chiefs. The Connaught men won the day and for some considerable time their dominance of the waters presented a constant threat to Thomond.

Conor's brother, Turlogh the prince of Thomond, was not idle either. When Cormac of Cashel (a bishop) attacked the city of Limerick he was later assassinated by Turlogh O'Brien. Conor died at Killaloe in AD 1142 and the next ruler on the throne of Munster was his brother Turlogh. Conor's only son Murtagh was installed as prince of Thomond. His brother Teigue Glé had to be satisfied with the lower ranking of Prince of Ormond.

Soon after Turlogh acceded to the throne of Munster he immediately set off on a raiding mission in Leinster. It would appear that the only way to a position of power as far as the Dalcassians were concerned was to subdue Leinster first. Then it was necessary to conquer either Ulster or Connaught. If the preceding were successful they would lead, in all probability, to the high kingship. It had worked for many of the descendants of Brian, and they were only following his example — although they proved less able than he.

Turlogh fought wars with such notables as the King of Meath, Diamuid McMurrough, and the usual Connaught chieftains. He also became a great antagonist of the MacCarthys in South Munster. While he and his army were battling the latter in the south, his own brother Teigue Glé, formed an alliance with Turlogh O'Connor. Teigue Glé was making a habit of turning against his kin and found little difficulty in allying the king of Meath and Diarmuid McMurrough to his cause.

Turlogh was returning from his raids on MacCarthy's territory when the allies of Teigue Glé ambushed him and his army in the parish of Emly in South Limerick. The overpowering numbers were too much for the Dalcassians and they suffered a devasting defeat. Some of the notable chiefs who fell in that battle were the O'Briens; the O'Kennedys; the O'Deas; the O'Shannons; the O'Quins; the O'Gradys; the O'Hogans; the Lynches; the O'Hehirs; the O'Hearns and the Dalcassian O'Neills. This victory gave Turlogh O'Connor undisputed control of Munster. Turlogh O'Brien was forced to flee to the north to save his own life. Teigue Glé was made Prince of Thomond with Dermot McCarthy becoming Prince of Desmond.

Shortly afterwards Murtagh MacLaughlin, of the northern Hy Nialls, marched south and scored some victories before entering Munster. He restored Turlogh O'Brien once more as Prince of Thomond. Teigue hastily left for he did not want to encounter the wrath of his brother Turlogh. Unfortunately for him another brother Dermod caught up with him and to render him ineffective he had his eyes pulled out. Teigue died in the following year 1154 as a result of this barbarous act.

In a jostling for positions between the northern O'Neills and O'Connor of Connaught, the powerless Turlogh was deposed and restored a few more times in Thomond, although towards the end of his reign he was known to have ruled with a very stern hand. He launched a final attack into South Munster in 1161. Many of the chiefs of the O'Donohues and O'Keefes were slain as was a son of Cormac MacCarthy, Prince of Desmond. When his own son, Mortagh, came of age he banished his father from the head of the clan. In 1167 the stormy career of Turlogh O'Brien came to an end when he died at Killaloe. Murtagh, his son, did not last long in office for he was killed by his cousin Conor O'Brien a year later. This cleared the way for a powerful man by the name of Donal More (The Great) O'Brien who was handed the Wand of Rule in 1168.

It might be as well to examine conditions prevailing in West Thomond (Clare) at that time. From the preceding accounts we note that the main preoccupation of the chiefs, princes, kings and noblemen alike was constant warfare to assert their authority. Local clans had laws — the Brehon Laws — for appointing their own rulers. Those laws could extend to areas as large as Munster. The main trouble stemmed from the fact that, to achieve the High Kingship of Ireland, one had to march on a circuit of the country with one's army. It was the only way to win the support of other provincial kings. If allegiance was not given voluntarily it was extracted by either crushing or plundering their territory. In rare cases a loose alliance might be formed. As we have seen it was usually the former method which was adopted.

There was the unique Irish system of clans banding together to hold their own districts. This led to a situation where a chief could only be safe in assuming that the main part of his army would always be formed by his own clansmen. It was not possible to expect long alliances from clans in other districts. Quite frequently a king would have to subdue, time and time again, the very same usurper in order to maintain his own position of power. This then was a very important factor in the Irish losing their territories to the next invader — the Normans.

Except for some churches and monasteries all other buildings of habitation were constructed from earth and wood with thatch roofs. Due to the constant commitment to warfare not much time could have been devoted to the advancement of living conditions. The vassals (mainly descendants of the Firbolg) were kept as tillers of the soil and working at handcrafts. In the unusual event of peace, the clansmen spent their energies on the chase. Hospitalities were occasionally exchanged amongst them. Great banquets took place quite frequently in the king's palace where the music of the harper was much appreciated. If real warfare could not be had there was always its popular substitute — a game of chess. Wine, beer and other luxuries were supplied to the Clare nobles by the Danes of Limerick. Produce of the county at the time was wool, hide, tallow and choice timber from the numerous forests. It is said that when the English later arrived they removed fine oaks from the forests of East Clare and used it for roofing Westminster Abbey in London.

The art of writing and learning was confined mainly to the monasteries. The vassals, craftsmen and even petty chiefs had little use for this important talent. In the monasteries many records were kept of the lives and events which were considered important. It is from these writings that most historical records are derived. Even though the Norse burned and destroyed many monasteries, and consequently many valuable documents, some notable works have survived.

It seems that religion had a somewhat different impact on the people then than it has had in recent times. War, murder and cruelty were pretty common occurrences. The O'Briens had a particularly effective though very barbarous method of dealing with people who were likely to hinder their aspirations. This was the custom of pulling out the eyes of their enemies, rendering them ineffective for life. In fact when Donal More O'Brien came to power his first inhuman act was to deprive his own brother, Brian Na Sleibhe, of his sight. It seems that brothers, cousins and adversaries alike were murdered as frequently as the need arose.

During the twelfth century the first semblance of villages and towns (outside of the Norse settlements) appeared throughout the land. We are told of Kincora (the town of Killaloe) being burned and looted by the Connaught clans. We note also that Tuamgraney was a population centre from quite early on. The reason for the growth of Killaloe as a town would have been its proximity to the palace of Kincora. It is likely that many of the king's subjects and attendants found it convenient to reside near their source of employment and also because it was safer to do so. Tuamgraney had a monastery and round tower at the time, and it was common for people to gravitate towards those religious settlements. In fact many of the centres of population in the county began their growth in this way. The present town of Ennis was later established around a monastic settlement early in the thirteenth century.

In previous pages we have read of many accounts of the type of warfare that the Irish were accustomed to. The reasons for such hostilities have also been mentioned, though not always explained. Mostly, the campaigns were spontaneous and elementary in execution.

Finally, the typical Irish fighting man should be looked at in order to understand some of the new problems he would encounter under more sophisticated warfare. A soldier of the period was equipped with a light axe, a sword, and perhaps a knife or a spear. These weapons were in daily use whether in time of war or peace, so most clansmen were quite adept at using them. Consequently, in close quarter combat a soldier would have to be pretty skilful to overcome an enemy who would be similarly equipped.

The armour of the early Irish was discussed by one Joseph Walker Cooper in findings which he made to the Rt Hon. Ely, Countess of Moyorre. His observations were based on coins and other data found in Queen's County in 1786. He noted that the helmet was of the open variety, possibly with ear flaps It could have been a general purpose piece of head gear used to keep the hair tidy when travelling through thick forest just as much as for deflecting blows during combat. This would have been in general use up to the tenth and eleventh centuries. Early helmets were made of animal hides. Later, when iron forgings came into general use, helmets were fashioned from that metal. However, if the Irishman's character has remained static down the centuries and if present-day hurlers are anything to go by, only the occasional and spasmodic wearing of the helmet would have been the order of the day.

A second defensive weapon used by the early Irish was the shield. Many of the illustrations of shields which have come down to us are seen to be circular in design, often embellished with Celtic designs brocaded on them. It appears that another type of shield would have been long and broad and would have resembled the Roman versions. As such they were often used for removing the wounded from the field of battle. Shields were firmly fixed to the hand and arm with thongs of leather. Body armour which dates before the tenth century has never been discovered. This would indicate that metals were not used in body armour prior to that period. This is in spite of folklore relating the exploits of Oisin of the Fianna in shining armour.

Weapons used on the offensive stemmed from those in everyday use, principally the spear and the axe. The spear, called Friach or Crannuibh, was more of a type of javelin. Approximately five feet in length it was pointed with a sharp flint stone or metal point. It was fixed to the hand by means of long leather thongs. The thongs helped in quick recovery for another throw.

The axe was an ancient weapon, developed by primitive man who used a flint or heavy stone head lashed to a wooden handle. By the eleventh century the axe had become more sophisticated and lethal. It was made from hammered iron and polished with a round cutting face of ample proportions. In the hands of those skilled axe men it was a devastating weapon that was capable of severing a limb with one heavy blow. Again, the axe would have been fixed to the wrist by means of heavy leather thongs. This helped in not dropping it during crucial moments of close quarter fighting.

A weapon developed solely for human combat was undoubtedly the sword. A long double edged knife, of the single hand and double hand variety, it was used as a slashing weapon for crowded fighting conditions. Brian Boru himself wielded a two-handed sword which was about six feet in length.

The Irish were most courageous fighters and never shirked their duty in time of battle. Certainly, the Dalcassian clans have a long history of daring warfare, they would not yield on the battlefield to any enemy. Yet, later on they were to be easily overcome — due mainly to their lack of tactics. This will be seen in the coming chapters when they take on new foes.

All the above-mentioned characteristics of the Irish kings and soldiers were detrimentally important factors when the Normans invaded the land. It was the lack of central Irish authority, their individual greed, primitive warfare and their inability to agree on any issue that was their ultimate downfall. Courage in itself could be used for or against them. Of itself courage could not plot their destiny.

When Donal More O'Brien became king of Thomond in AD 1168 he immediately indulged in the usual civil strife favoured by his predecessors. He had numerous battles with the king of Connaught, Rory O'Connor. O'Connor had some useful allies, particularly O'Ruarck of Breffney — a combination at times that proved more than a handful for the O'Briens. Looking around for allies of his own Donal More eventually turned to a recent invader who was capable of giving him the military support he was seeking. This turning to the invader, even though at the time it was not considered a long-term threat, proved to be serious mistake for the Irish kings. It was to considerably alter the lifestyle in the country, eventually working its way into that most difficult of all territories to penetrate — the Dalcassian homelands.

Chapter 5

Kings and Normans (1169 — 1342)

Though not strictly Clare history, the following Irish history does have a distinct bearing on subsequent events in the county. It will be briefly looked at for that reason.

Dermot MacMurrough's squabbles with O'Ruarck, Prince of Breffney, ended in the former fleeing to England. There he sought aid from King Henry II who, out of sheer speculation, provided him with sixty men in armour. They landed in Leinster and managed to remain there without hindrance. Little did MacMurrough realise but Henry had more devious plans for the control of Ireland than he (MacMurrough) could possibly imagine. In May 1169 Robert FitzStephens and Maurice FitzGerald, both English Normans, landed at the creek of Barrow in County Wexford. Their army consisted of thirty knights, sixty men in suits of mail and three hundred archers. On 23 August in the same year twelve hundred more fighting men under Strongbow landed near Waterford. Those combined forces of experienced mercenaries immediately stormed Waterford, Wexford and Dublin. With their highly mobile knights on well-bred fighting horses, their soldiers covered in protective mail and wearing conical helmets, they looked and indeed were, a superior fighting force.

It is worth noting here the introduction of archers for the first time into Ireland. The English, who had perfected the use of arrows in fighting battles, had a distinct advantage over the Irish. Indeed, we are told that this type of warfare was to infuriate the Irish. They regarded the bow and arrow as offensive (more of an insult) and despicable and not at all in accordance with decent fighting.

Militarily, the Normans were very successful. They met only occasional resistance from the high king, Rory O'Connor. He was hampered in his attempts against the invaders by the troublesome O'Brien of Thomond. So much so, he found it necessary to command his clans to attack the kingdom from end to end. The O'Kellys continually plundered Ormond while the clans from west Connaught ravaged the kingdom from Galway Bay to the Shannon. These assaults were encouraged by O'Connor because it kept O'Brien out of his hair. Although often caught unawares, the MacNamaras, O'Liddys, O'Gradys, and the O'Moloneys, MacInerneys, MacGraths etc., fought some valiant rearguard actions against the Connaught men. These clashes left many of the Galway chiefs dead on the battlefield. On retreating, the Connaught clans burned the bridge at Killaloe. The Dalcassians were therefore confined within the county for a time.

Once again due to lack of Irish unity, O'Connor failed to get in a telling blow against the Normans. In a short while Strongbow was claiming sovereignty of Leinster. Fearing that his underlords were becoming too powerful Henry decided to come over from England and conquer the country for himself.

Henry II of England set sail from Milford Haven with a fleet of two hundred and forty small vessels containing about four thousand men. He landed near Waterford on 18 October 1171, and immediately Strongbow handed over the city to him. Soon he was marching to Cashel where he produced a Bull from the Pope. With this Bull he hoped to obtain the support of the Church. Most of the local princes submitted to him, including Donal More O'Brien. He formally handed over control of the city of Limerick to Henry, which was an acknowledgement that Henry was his liege. Seemingly, O'Brien did not place unusual importance in this submission for we note that life continued much as before in Thomond. Perhaps a prince like O'Brien saw no difference in being underlord to an Irish or an English king. However, this act of acknowledgement by the Munster chiefs is important because it was the first footing gained by the English in Munster. After a short time Henry left Ireland. He was summoned by the Pope to answer for the murder of Thomas Becket.

Strongbow was determined to establish his authority in Munster as he had done in Leinster. With this purpose in mind he marched into the province at the head of an army of Normans and Danes. Donal More O'Brien was waiting for him near Thurles in County Tipperary. The forces met in an immediate head-on battle. Four of the Norman knights were slain and an estimated seventeen hundred fighting men were also killed in the battle. The success of this great conflict can be attributed to the fact that the Dalcassian and Connaught clans teamed up for once and were found fighting shoulder to shoulder. Had the Irish followed up this policy at the time, no doubt they would have easily routed the invader from the country.

This defeat shocked Strongbow. He recalled Raymond Le Gros and his army from Wales and sent them to the city of Limerick which was the O'Brien capital at the time. The intrepid Le Gros forded the river Shannon in the shallow place where St John's castle now stands. Because the defenders had felled the bridges the appearance of Le Gros and his men caught them unawares and most of them fled the city in panic. Donal O'Brien immediately rode to Castleconnell where he accused his own cousin of treachery. For this alleged betrayal he put out the eyes of his own kinsmen, Dermot and Turlogh O'Brien. He also killed O'Connor a son of the Prince of Corcomore who happened to be in the house at the time.

After that Rory O'Connor, the generally recognised king of Ireland, paid tribute to Henry as his king with certain rights in Ireland. Rory was not pleased with the support he was receiving from Donal More and in retribution he ravaged Thomond, chasing Donal More to Limerick and from there to Cashel. He was intercepted at Cashel by Raymond Le Gros and some clans from Ossory. Although they fought valliantly the Dalcassians had to finally submit to Le Gros. O'Brien and Le Gros retired to Limerick where they spent some time working out a solution to their problems. Word came that Strongbow had died and this prompted Le Gros to depart at once for Dublin. He left Donal More in charge of the city. O'Brien soon became disenchanted with the English lords and their lust for conquest. No sooner had Le Gros left his sight when O'Brien set Limerick alight. His reason was that the city would always be a stronghold for foreigners and it was better destroyed.

In the year 1178 the Dalcassians saw fit to resume their ancestral struggle with the Eoghanachts in South Munster. The Thomond warriors scoured the province in search of their traditional enemy. As well as fleeing into every remote corner of Munster, the MacCarthys, O'Collins and O'Donovans escaped even into west Thomond itself. This accounts for some of those family names in the county at present.

It would be interesting to note at this turning point in Clare history the localities occupied by the principal clans. This can be done with greater accuracy since they began to be known by certain family names, though the old prized title of Dalcassian belonged then and ever since to all alike.

The O'Briens, as the dominant clan, had secured land in many parts of the county, the principal area being the territory round the palace of Kincora, the greatest part of the barony of Inchiquin, part of Tradaree, and the district along the Atlantic from Dunbeg by Miltown-Malbay to Ennistymon. The Mac-Namaras, whose chief was hereditary Lord Marshal of Thomond, owned nearly all of the eastern part of the county, from Tulla and Broadford on the north out of which they drove the O'Kennedys down nearly to the Shannon. In the days of their power their chiefs were styled respectively Princes of East and West Clancuilean.

The O'Deas owned the country called Dysert O'Dea, while between them and the O'Brien's land at Kilfarboy, and the O'Gormans and O'Donnells of Clonderlaw, through Inagh, Clouna, Kilnamona, Kilmaley (called Breintír, no man's land), were fixed the MacClanchys (stronghold, Caher MacClancy), the O'Hehirs and the MacBruidins or Brodys, hereditary historians of Thomond. The O'Quins had the beautiful though not extensive territory around Corofin, while all the rest of north-west Clare out to the ocean, belonged chiefly to the O'Loughlins and the O'Connors. The O'Hallorans owned the country south-west of Tulla towards Ennis, while the O'Moloneys had the district north of it to the borders of Galway. Between these and the O'Briens at Kincora, along the bay of Scariff south and south-west of it, were the O'Liddys, the O'Gradys, the MacInerneys, the O'Malones and others of less note because they were less in number.

There are many more lesser known names, with the same origins and inheritors of the same soul-stirring traditions. The names are here still; the people bearing them cling yet to the lands owned by their forefathers since long before the Christian era. Unfortunately many of the great clan leaders were to desert their clans in the interest of power and wealth much in the fashion of the English conqueror who influenced them.

Time passed without anything of much significance happening until the year 1185. At that time John, son of Henry II, came with an army into Ireland. He marched on Thomond with intention of subduing O'Brien. The Dalcassians met his army as soon as he entered the kingdom and a great battle followed. Much of John's army were slaughtered in the fight and the young prince was forced to retreat in haste.

Later that same year the Normans meddled in the affairs of the claimants to the Connaught throne. They induced O'Brien to side with them against his old enemies and foolishly he was only too glad to oblige. He joined in the plunder of Connaught with his usual zeal.

To indicate the trend of the times, the Norman/English grouping made a truce with the O'Connors of Connaught shortly afterwards. They then turned round and marched into Thomond where they burned and plundered Killaloe, ransacked and destroyed churches and houses. These tactics of switching their allegiance to different Irish chiefs by the English Normans were carried out regularly and with devastating effect. In this way the foreigner was encouraging more strife than was already there. Undoubtedly this weakened the Irish as a collective force. The inability of the native Irish to pull together was truly a disastrous characteristic.

To show what could be accomplished one particular incident is worth noting. John De Courcey (a Norman) crossed the Shannon with a huge army, in a bid to subdue the entire western half of the country. Such was the alarm of the clans that they forgot all else save defending their own territories. Without hesitation, the Dalcassian and Connaught clans allied themselves together and ambushed the invading army in the Corlieu mountains. This large force of fierce fighting men literally slashed the Norman army to pieces. Indeed the survivors were quite lucky to escape as the Dalcassians made a bold attempt to cut off their retreat. After this victory the clans returned to their homes amid a great welcome. Thereafter they set about replacing recent war damages to their houses and towns.

In spite of these reversals the foreigner was not content at being shut out of the west, especially when he had the east of the country under his control. By 1192 the English had mustered all their Norman fighting men in the country at the time. They descended in great numbers on Ormond and surged across the Shannon at Killaloe. Their plan was to sweep through the heart of West Thomond (Clare) and capture the territory by attacking its very core. In the flat plains south of Killaloe the Dalcassians regrouped and stood fast. Eventually, they succeeded in pushing the Normans back across the Shannon. The foreigners were forced to retreat to Thurles, with the Dalcassians in hot pursuit. Thurles was also the scene of their first famous victory over the Normans. Once again the Dalcassians repeated their earlier success with another crushing defeat of the enemy. The Thomond army was unable to pursue the remainder of the Normans into Leinster because they feared that the Irish of Leinster would attack them. Had the Irish clans in Leinster realised the significance of this great event and sided with the Dalcassians, the foreign threat could have been broken forever at that point. It is difficult to understand their attitude in not being able to compromise for their own common good. (However, one supposes that the concept of a nation was not as well developed then as it is today). Donal More O'Brien had to be satisfied with ridding his own county of the Norman/English menace. He and his army then returned to Thomond where they lived in relative peace for the next few years.

Quin Abbey, Augustin'an. Founded in 1350 by the MacNamaras.
Pope Eugenius IV permitted friars of the strict observance there in 1433. Built on the site of a Norman castle.

Towards the end of his twenty-six years' reign as king, Donal contented himself with building churches for the diocese. The present church at Killaloe was built by him at that time. He also commissioned the Cathedral of St Mary in Limerick. In his reign over the Dalcassians he certainly established their authority and independence. The name which has stuck with him, Donal More (The Great), was truly justified in that he was the most powerful man in Munster at the time. Indeed, at times, he was acknowledged by many to be the true king of all Ireland.

Donal More died in 1194. His oldest son Murtagh Dall took his place. Unfor-

ENNIS.—ITS SOUTH-EAST PROSPECT.

A. The Abbey.   D. Hall of the Assizes.   B. Lenthall's, the chief Inn.

A view of the emerging town of Ennis, 1680. (DINELEY'S JOURNAL, 1680).

tunately, Murtagh was soon captured by the English and deprived of his sight by them (hence the name 'Dall' which means sightless). Murtagh's brother, Conor Roe, was then inaugurated at Magh Adhair as the new king. It appears that there was no authoritative person at that time strong enough to hold the position for in 1198 Conor Roe was dethroned. Finally, it was Donal More's third son, Donogh Cairbreach O'Brien, who firmly entrenched himself in the Thomond seat in 1201.

The English were still endeavouring to gain a foothold in West Thomond. Some minor incursions were made by them with a view to establishing a fortress in the area. In an effort to strengthen his forces in Ireland and to finally conquer the country, King John landed with a large army in 1210. Immediately Donogh Cairbreach acknowledged him as supreme king in Ireland. That led to John bestowing the kingship of Thomond on Donogh. In tribute to the English monarch, Donogh paid one thousand marks and a yearly sum of one hundred pounds. Another concession given was that the English would be allowed to build two castles in Thomond. One was at Roscrea (in County Tipperary) and the second was at Killaloe. Donogh found it necessary to have a strong ally like John because his own cousin Mortogh was contesting the kingship. But the presence of the English in Limerick was repugnant to Donogh, and he moved his place of residence to where the present town of Ennis now stands.

The Ennis area was not a significant place until Donogh moved there around 1216. Therefore it could be claimed that Donogh Cairbreach O'Brien was the founder of the town. He built a large earthen and stone fort on a site near where the present Clonroad bridge now stands. Donogh is also the direct ancestor of the kings and earls of Thomond, and the Viscounts of Clare, and the titled families of Inchiquin. He could be termed the first of the O'Briens as we know them today.

In 1224 a fierce civil war took place in Connaught between the members of the O'Connor clans. The struggle developed over the question of leadership. Donogh was an uncle of Hugh O'Connor, one of the pretenders to the throne. The Dalcassians grouped with Hugh's soldiers and they received backing from an English contingent whose policy was to promote disorder at all times. The O'Neill clan, who were on the other side, were forced to retreat because of the strength of the alliance formed by O'Connor and the Dalcassians. It was an easy opportunity for the Dalcassians who plundered all before them before retiring to their own territory.

In a retaliatory action some years later the Connaught clans, aided and abetted by the English, launched an assault on north Clare. The English supplied expertise on the field and because of their armoured soldiers and some cavalry they succeeded in overpowering the Clare clans. Donogh O'Brien's leadership was criticised in this engagement, but credit must be given to the experienced mercenaries of the English. This was to be the last disturbance of its type for some time on Thomond soil. Until he died in 1242 it seems that Donogh was not involved in anything else of note.

Conor, a son of Donogh O'Brien, became king after his father died. Since the English were in permanent garrison near Killaloe (the old seat of the Dalcassian kings) Clonroad was preferred as the new residence of the O'Briens.

In 1247 Conor built a Franciscan monastery quite near his palace at Clonroad. As can still be seen from the present-day ruins in Abbey Street, Ennis, it is an imposing structure. In the years that followed the abbey became renowned as a seat of learning and a place of worship. The commissioning of this monastery by Conor ensured the growth of a population centre there. Clonroad (the meadow of the long rowing) can be regarded as the capital of the county ever since. An explanation of the term 'meadow of the long rowing' may be found to be interesting. The river Fergus spilled into the marshy area at Clonroad and there was no clearcut channel as we know it today, instead strong reeds and long grass abounded. As can be imagined it was quite difficult and time consuming pulling oars through an area the size of the present town of Ennis. Hence it was a marshy meadow that required long rowing to traverse it in a boat.

Conor O'Brien was not without his problems as we next find him engaging the English of Thomond in battle in 1257. He is credited with killing a substantial number of them in skirmishes about the county. Those victories encouraged other Irish princes to do battle against the recent invader.

A meeting was convened by all Irish provincial kings at Cael Uisce on Lough Erne in 1258. This was a significant attempt to decide on a combined strategy against the enemy. Conor was unable to attend so he sent his son, Teigue. It was agreed by the assembly as a whole that the country would benefit best from having one ruler only — one who would have at his command a national army. The men in contention for this position were O'Neill from the north, and O'Brien from Thomond. O'Neill was the favourite but the young Teigue would not yield his father's claim. This was a momentous decision in Irish history. Had O'Brien backed O'Neill there was an excellent possibility that the united Irish would have rid the country of the English. However, it was not easy for the young son of Conor to relinquish the O'Brien claim on the High Kingship. The most genuine explanation would be that it was difficult for any O'Brien to believe that they were unworthy of the High Kingship, given their historical association with that office. A more shallow reason for his decision would be that he was aware that men were dying daily for less serious discretions; it would have been difficult for him to face home with a creditable explanation. The tendency of the time was to act first and ask questions later. He became known as Teigue Cael-Uisce after the event. Teigue died in the following year without assuming a position of power.

Realising that this would be an advantageous time to attack the Irish, the English in south Munster crossed the Shannon into West Thomond. But they were halted by Conor and his Dalcassians at Kilbarron, near Feakle. They completely routed the English and killed many of them. A son of Conor, Brian Roe, avenged this latest attack by wiping out to the last man the English garrison at Castleconnell in Limerick.

Conor now saw fit to reduce to submission some of his own clans in Thomond. He visited the clans of north-east Clare and of Ormond, and he extracted many tributes from them. Then he crossed over to the Burren where he met stubborn resistance from the O'Loughlins, the O'Deas, the O'Connors and the O'Hehirs. When he encountered Conor Carach O'Loughlin at the wood of the Suidaine in the parish of Drumcreehy, a violent battle ensued. Conor O'Brien lost the battle and his life, and from it gained the name of Conor-na-Suidaine. He was buried (1267) in the abbey of Corcomroe, which had been built some time previously by his grandfather Donal More O'Brien. A monument over his tomb — a reclining figure in limestone — can still be seen there.

The reclining figure of Conor O'Brien in Corcomroe Abbey, slain at the Battle of Suidaine, 1267. Abbey dates from the late twelfth century, founded by Donal More O'Brien.

Brian Roe O'Brien became the next king of Thomond. He, like his predecessors, busied himself chastising friend and foe alike. By now we would assume these events to be commonplace and will, out of interest, dwell a little more on foreign acquisitions in Clare.

The English built a castle at Clarecastle (remains of the ruin can still be seen near the present bridge) so that they could better hold their gains in the county. Its construction coincided with the rise of Brian Roe to power. It was called Clar Atha or 'the boarded ford' and from it the county took its name, Clare. The present village of Clarecastle derived its name from the same source.

A nephew of Brian Roe, Turlogh, was next to assert his right to the throne. Brian Roe was forced to seek military assistance from Thomas De Clare, a son of the Earl of Gloucester. De Clare and Brian Roe marched on Clonroad but found that Turlogh was away soliciting support in the territory of Corcobaskin. Finding that he had a foothold in West Thomond the Englishman, De Clare, rebuilt Bunratty castle (1277) to hold the lands he had just acquired. Later that same year, De Clare had Brian Roe treacherously and cruelly killed. Brian Roe was enticed to Bunratty on some pretext or another. Religious oaths were solemnly sworn by De Clare that no harm would come to him. When he was inside the walls of Bunratty, the Dalcassian prince was immediately made prisoner. Brian Roe was subjected to much torture. Finally, he had to endure the horrific death of being drawn apart between two horses.

In the following year Turlogh, the then ruling king, routed the English from the county, with the exception of a small contingent in Bunratty castle. Regrettably, in doing so he was forced to burn St Finghin's church in Quin, where a party of them had taken refuge.

Something of particular interest was undertaken by Turlogh at this time. He built the first Irish stone castle, after the Norman fashion, on the peninsula near the island of Inis (Ennis). Even though the Norman technique of holding land with impregnable fortresses had been obvious to the Irish for one hundred years, this was the first time that one of them put it to practical use. Unfortunately, that same castle was destroyed three hundred years later with not a trace of it remaining today. Stones from the castle were used in the construction of a new house for a Mr Gore elsewhere in the town of Ennis. Before his death on 10 April 1306, Turlogh made many improvements to the abbey at Clonroad. He is one of a number of Thomond monarchs laid to rest there.

In the following years there were many battles between the Thomond kings, Donogh O'Brien, Donal Bawn O'Brien and De Clare and his Irish allies. Donogh and Donal Bawn suffered a heavy defeat in the battle of Dysert O'Dea at the hands of Murtagh O'Brien. In 1311, Dermot, a grandson of Brian Roe, was inaugurated as king at Magh Adhair. This was in opposition to the legal heir Murtagh who was his cousin. De Clare continued to stir up the pot of Irish turmoil, but finally his day of reckoning came. While leading a large English following through the county, De Clare was utterly defeated on 13 May 1318 near Dysert O'Dea. A local chief slew De Clare and the body was hacked to pieces in a fit of rage. De Clare's widow burned Bunratty castle (then a wooden structure) and fled to England with as many valuables as she could carry.

This broke the English dominance in the county for nearly two centuries. After Dysert O'Dea the English began to realise that Thomond was not the easiest place to conquer. Brian Bawn and Mahon of Inchiquin retired to East Thomond, while Murtagh reigned as the undisputed Prince of Thomond. He died in 1343 after a successful reign of more than thirty years.

The MacNamaras were growing in strength and power at about this time. It is noted that they held much of the territory of east Clare, including the lower Fergus to the Glendaree Hills, from Tulla to Broadford and down to the Shannon.

How had the local clans fared against the more sophisticated fighting Normans from England? The Dalcassians got the upperhand in most contests, but this was probably due to superior numbers, rather than to tactics of any kind. It is evident that the clans had scant regard for their own personal safety. More than likely, it was this trait that cost them most of the losses they suffered. They refused to wear helmets, mail or armour. Their heart's delight was a good old fashioned hand-to-hand battle in a large clearing. With regard to personal armour, they appeared to disregard it as being of little consequence.

According to one historian, when the Irish encountered a man in armour on horseback, they preferred to use their steel axe. Its striking feature was a blade which had been adapted from the Danes. The weapon was held in one hand with the thumb extended along the shaft. Since they were unable to reach to the head of the attacking soldier on horseback, they would strike a swift downward blow into the rider's thigh. A well delivered blow would sever the leg from the body. This resulted in the limb falling to one side while the body fell lifeless at the other side of the horse!

Irish fighting men of the time also carried a few short spears and two javelins. When all else failed, he would not hesitate to use stones from the ground. Instead of armour the Irish soldier fought in a linen tunic. In sharp contrast to him the Norman soldier came well equipped with large pikes, swords and a back-up unit of archers. They would hold any territory taken by constructing large castles or fortresses, in elevated locations, if at all possible. Later, the Irish, and especially the MacNamaras in Clare, adopted this tactic to good effect in their own county. Indeed it was to become the county with more castles than any other in Ireland.

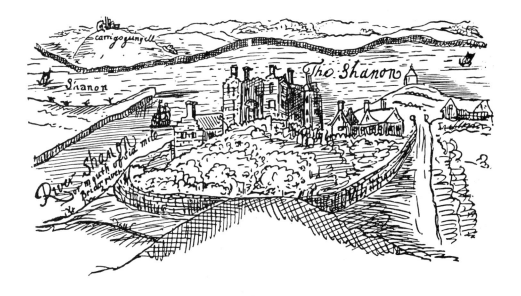

Dineley's sketch of Bunratty Castle in 1680.

Chapter 6

English Takeover
(1343 — 1580)

During this period many of the usual local disorders took place, but much of it is without significance. Items which directly influence the course of history, shall only be considered.

On the death of Murtagh, Brian took over as the new king in Thomond. He ruled peacefully until he was treacherously slain in 1350 by Clan Keogh, east of the Shannon. Dermot reigned next without registering anything of note, until Mahon Moinmoy wrested the seat by force from him. He wore the crown with some dissension. Notably, he was responsible for imposing a yearly levy of 'Black Rent' on the English of Munster. When Mahon died in 1367 his brother Turlogh Maoel was next in line. His rule lasted only three years because he was driven out by his nephew Brian Catha-an-Aenagh.

Turlogh crossed into Limerick to seek aid from Garrett, Earl of Desmond, who received him favourably. Before Turlogh, with his Irish and Norman/Irish allies, could invade West Thomond they found that Brian, at the head of a large force of O'Briens and MacNamaras had advanced to meet them near Croom. Many of the Desmond men were slain in a battle in which their army was heavily defeated. John FitzNicholas, Sir Thomas FitzJohn, the Earl of Desmond and many other nobles were taken prisoner. The Dalcassians also sacked Limerick city and left Sheeda Cam MacNamara in charge of it. He was later murdered by some of the English who remained on in the city.

In 1394, Richard II of England landed in the country with a force of about thirty-four thousand fighting men. With this huge army in evidence, the Irish princes, Brian O'Brien included, showed good sense in paying mock homage to Richard. There was no evident effect of Richard's army in Thomond and seemingly life went on as before. Brian died in 1399, ending his reign peace-fully.

The year 1350 is given as the year of construction for the beautiful Francis-can Abbey at Quin. Its well preserved ruins are a notable attraction even at the present day. The cloister was commissioned by Sheeda Cam MacNamara who requested that the Abbey was to be his own burial place.

Brian's brother, Conor, was the elected prince of Thomond, and ruled with-out hindrance until his death in 1426. Teigue-na-Glenmore became the new prince but he governed without us learning anything more about him. There was juggling for power during the next few years between first, Mahon Dall (the blind), then Turlogh Bog (the soft), until 1459. A two year reign by Mahon's son Donogh ended with Teigue-an-Chomhaid (of Coad on the lake of Inchiquin) in control. Teigue built a beautiful castle residence by the lake of Inchiquin.

During this time the English presence became weak around Thomond. The O'Briens continued to enforce the Black Rent on the English, which their ancestor Mahon Moinmoy had initiated. The rent was in payment for land occupied. Such were things at the time, that Teigue considered himself in a position to challenge for the high kingship of the country. He attempted to assert his claim in the fashion originally started by the first O'Brien — Brian Boru of the Tributes.

To begin with, Teigue brought a huge army of his followers into South Munster and gained control of the entire present county of Limerick. He imposed a yearly tribute of sixty marks on the chiefs there, to be payable forever to him. Being satisfied that Limerick was well and truly subdued, he moved on to the old battlegrounds of Ossory and Leinster where he scored more successes. As a hard winter was drawing in he was obliged to return to West Thomond by way of Limerick. This campaign had established him as the strongest ruler in Leath Mogha, the southern half of the country. Had he not died that very same year (1466) we might have seen a return of the Ard Righ in Ireland.

Conor-na-Srona (of the Great Nose), a brother of Teigue, became the next king. His reign started with his relative, MacWilliam of Clanrickard, and himself waging war against the O'Kellys of Hy Many, the O'Donnells and the Mac-William Eighter. The Dalcassians won a major battle against their neighbours near the city of Galway. Thereafter peace prevailed in the county for more than twenty years.

In 1483, Mahon O'Griffy, Bishop of Killaloe, died and was buried in an island at the mouth of the Fergus. His body was interned in the Abbey of the Canons Regular of St Augustine on that island. From this, the island derived its present name of Canon Island.

As the fifteenth century drew to a close, the Earl of Kildare became enraged with the Dalcassians. They had supported a spurious claimant to the Ormond seat in preference to the legitimate heir, who happened to be married to the Earl's sister. The Earl brought a large army to the Shannon and crossed into MacNamara territory. First they captured the castle of Ballycullen and left a garrison there. They then marched on to Conor O'Brien's fortress at Clonroad. The hastily summoned clans cut off the marchers and confronted the invaders and their allies near Quin. At Ballyhickey castle the forces met and did battle. After a very stern encounter the Claremen emerged as victors. This routing of the invader from the county left Thomond without threat of takeover for some more years. The last important act of Conor-na-Srona was his capturing of Fineen MacNamara's castle near Quin. After a particularly long rule of thirty years, Conor died in 1496.

As we move into the sixteenth century it is noticeable that the original Dalcassian clans were still in possession of their long held territories. The

O'Briens and the MacNamaras were the principal clans both in numbers and authority. Most of Kincora and district, belonged to the O'Briens. They also owned the Barony of Inchiquin, some parts of Tradaree, lands on the west coast around Doonbeg, Miltown and Ennistymon.

By this time the MacNamaras were building stone castles all over their lands. They became the possessors of the greatest number of castles in West Thomond. As timber was still plentiful, it can be assumed that many of the houses of vassals and the lowly ranked, were constructed with this material. Although the castles and churches were large enough, the architecture was more practical than elaborate. Clothing was certainly crude enough, being made from hides and rough wool. The main pastimes were fencing, hurling, athletic contests, music and storeytelling.

After Conor-na-Srona, came Turlogh Gilla Dubh (of the dark complexion). He reigned for only three years and three months and nothing of interest is recorded of him. His successor was his nephew Turlogh Don (of the yellow hair) who immediately set about burning and looting the city of Limerick.

Shortly after that event an uncle of Turlogh O'Brien, MacWilliam of Clanrickard, seized some castles belonging to the O'Kelly's of Hy Many. The O'Kellys called on the Lord Justice Kildare, who had no love for Clanrickard, to assist them. Garret, the Lord Justice Kildare, brought an army from the east and north consisting of Hugh Roe O'Donnell and his son. It also included a group of Connacians, and MacDermot, Lord of Moylurg, and his followers. These and many lesser clans made a forced march on Clanrickard. MacWilliam requested assistance from Turlogh O'Brien and his clans, from Mulrony O'Carroll, Lord of Ely, and from many more of the Ormond clans.

The forces met at Knockdoe, eight miles north-west of Galway, on 19 August 1504. There were an estimated two thousand of the Thomond troops killed in a protracted and bitter struggle. Little quarter was given or taken during the course of the battle and what few English archers were in attendance, stayed well clear of the main fighting arena. No English fell, but no doubt they were delighted at the sight of the Irish weakening each other in so terrible a feud. Such were the cries and clamour from the hotly contesting armies, that the din could be heard for a good distance off. Finally the Dalcassians and Clanrickard had to withdraw, even though losses on both sides were about equal.

This contest greatly weakened the Thomond clans. They soon realised that they had put their ability to hold their lands against the English in great jeopardy, by so diminishing their numbers. Fortunately the English were also without depth of strength and no attack on Thomond came from that quarter.

In the year 1508 Lord Kildare was back in Munster attempting to consolidate English rule in that province. Having subdued Cork without much effort, he marched on Limerick. From their peninsula kingdom across the Shannon, the Dalcassians were carefully monitoring his movements. Massed on the banks of the river were the huge MacNamara clans, proud, fierce and warlike. Of course the O'Briens were much in evidence, as were the O'Deas, O'Hehirs, O'Quins, MacInerneys and indeed all the other clans of West Thomond. MacWilliam of Clanrickard, as well he might, assembled his entire fighting force and came to the assistance of Turlogh.

Lord Kildare destroyed the wooden bridge of Portoroise, which forded the Shannon near Castleconnell. But the Dalcassians crossed the Shannon at Killaloe and made a day-long march down the south bank. They came quite near to Kildare's forces at dusk and then made camp. The opposing forces were billeted so close together that they could hear each other speaking in the night. Early next day Kildare withdrew towards Limerick, probably looking for a vantage point from which to fight. However, the Thomond and Connaught clans caught up with the enemy. In a full day's battle of heavy fighting, the English and their Irish allies suffered a narrow defeat. This victory left a lasting impression in the mind of Lord Kildare. He realised it was in no way beneficial to do battle in Thomond or Clanrickard. Lord Kildare and his son who succeeded him, never ventured back to these territories again.

From 1510 to 1522 life was comparatively uneventful in Thomond under Turlogh Don. In 1523 a small contingent was sent to the north of the country, to assist O'Neill against O'Donnell. O'Neill and the Dalcassians did not unite properly and as a result O'Neill lost nine hundred men. The Dalcassians effected a hasty, if unlikely, retreat back to Thomond.

It is worth noting the following event, which took place around 1524. Prince Butler, Lord of Ormond, made war on Thomond and met a force of Dalcassians under Teigue, son of Turlogh Don, near Cashel. When the young prince, Teigue, was struck down by the shot of a ball, the Dalcassians retreated carrying his body. This is the first occasion that the use of firearms is recorded. Teigue's body was returned to Ennis where it was interned in the Abbey of his ancestors. His father, Turlogh Don, died in 1528 and he was laid to rest beside his son in the Abbey of Ennis.

Beside Teigue, Reignault who was the wife of Turlogh, had many more sons. Most famous of these were Conor, who was the succeeding prince; and Murrogh par Excellence, the Tanist. From Conor are descended the Earls of Thomond. It is from Murrogh that the Barons of Inchiquin, the O'Briens of Dromoland, those of Blatherwycke, Glencolumbkille and many others, are traced.

Conor then became King of Thomond and was married twice. Donogh the Fat, was the only son of his first marriage to Arabella de Burgh, a daughter of MacWilliam of Clanrickard. From his second marriage to a sister of the Earl of Thomond, he was father to Sir Donal O'Brien and Sir Turlogh.

About this time, Henry VIII of England was becoming concerned over the close relationship that the Earl of Kildare was attaining with the Irish. He summoned the Earl to London and imprisoned him in the Tower. His son, Silken Thomas Fitzgerald, panicked and organised a rebellion in Ireland. However, it did not receive adequate support from the Irish in Leinster. When Skeffington came to Ireland, he had little difficulty in quelling the revolt.

Silken Thomas fled to the safety of Thomond. Such was the strength and independence of the kingdom in those days, that he felt it was the only sure place of refuge. His family and friends were guests at the castle in Clonroad for six months.

Later he surrendered to Lord Grey and was sent to the Tower in London. After a time, he, and five of his uncles were executed. A twelve year old son of Silken Thomas remained behind in the castle at Clonroad, under the pro-

Norman style tower house. These structures had their staircases and roofs demolished in the seventeenth century by the Commissioners for overthrowing and demolishing castles in Connaught and Clare. Picture shows Dysert Castle. Restored in 1986 and opened to the public.

tection of Conor O'Brien. But this purge of the Geraldine power in Ireland by Henry VIII had considerably weakened the Irish position. They were now prone to being subjugated completely by the English Monarch.

Henry was not happy with the contempt shown for his rule in Ireland by the O'Briens. He sent the Lord Deputy, Lord Leonard Grey towards Thomond to extract some measure of submission from the clans there. The Lord Deputy came as far as Limerick and took the castle of Carrigoguinnell in 1536. Lord Grey received token aid from Donogh O'Brien in capturing that fortress. Noticeably, some Irish nobility were by then showing a willingness to defect to the English side. The following year saw the English forces campaigning once again to take Thomond. Ormond relinquished its territory without opposition and indeed in June of that year, the Danish and English settlers of Limerick gladly handed over that city to the Lord Deputy.

Conor O'Brien met the Lord Deputy at Limerick and some type of arrangement was made between them. O'Brien undertook to chastise his rebellious brother, Murrogh the Tanist, who was probably being supported by the MacNamaras.

The Lord Deputy was allowed to march through West Thomond towards Clare Castle, where he took Murrogh's castle there. It was the first time that the Dalcassians had seen that fearful war machine — the cannon — and resistance was minimal. The English force pushed on towards Galway, bypassing the O'Brien fortress at Clonroad. They were allowed to pass unmolested by the O'Deas through their lands in north Clare.

This was the first substantial footing by the English in West Thomond since the days of De Clare back in the early part of the thirteenth century. Conor had in effect given a partial submission to the English. But with the Ormond princes in East Thomond completely capitulating, it was becoming increasingly difficult for the O'Briens to hold West Thomond. Conor died two years later in 1539. He died with the distinction, of still being ruler of Thomond and significantly, the last of the descendants of the great Brian Boru to do so.

Until that time the people enjoyed the freedom of the land in their own areas. The Church also had its own measure of independence with the will to receive gifts of land and monasteries from the nobility. In order to have complete control of the people, the English next introduced their own system of land ownership and their own Church laws. On 1 May 1537, the English monarch was henceforth declared to be the head of the Church in Ireland.

Murrogh, like all the Irish princes, was bribed by gifts of land and titles for his own family and descendants, if he would relinquish his native power. He travelled to Greenwich, where he was made Earl of Thomond on Sunday 1 July 1542. The title of Baron of Ibricken was bestowed on his nephew Donogh.

Soon, the rest of the Thomond chiefs began to realise that their days as rulers were numbered, and they also followed the example of the O'Briens. Sheeda MacNamara looked for a peerage and requested his lands be transferred over to him in the English system of fee simple. The latter wish was granted but he was made a knight instead of the higher title of peerage.

Grants of Church land were made by the English to its new nobility, the land having been acquired by the recent suppression of the monasteries. Until Murrogh died in 1551, the English made no other impression in Thomond. But the die had been cast when the English titles were accepted. The changing over to individual ownership of land, from the Irish system of clan ownership, paved the way for effective English control.

Donogh O'Brien became the new Earl of Thomond, a position that was made hereditary by King Edward VI. The Earl's immediate relatives now realised that they would have no chance of assuming power on his death because of this new English system of the line descending through the eldest son. Donal and Turlogh O'Brien attacked Donogh in his fortress at Clonroad during the dead of night. Donogh managed to escape to his tower but was gravely wounded in the process. The enraged brothers then plundered and burned the town of Ennis. A few weeks later, on Passion Saturday, Donogh died and was succeeded by Donal O'Brien, the ancestor of the Ennistymon O'Briens. No sooner had Donal taken control, when he struck out to re-assert Dalcassian superiority. He made raids into Leinster and marched home by Clanrickard, where he did considerable damage to castles and livestock. But his usurpage did not go unnoticed by the English. In 1558 the Earl of Sussex, with a very well equipped army, marched into Thomond. Donal did not resist and the castles of Bunratty, Clare (Clarecastle) and Clonroad were seized.

Donal and his family were forced to flee to Maguire of Fermanagh for protection. His nephew, Conor, and old protagonist, was made an Earl. Conor renounced all the ancient Dalcassian rights in return for the English feudal rights of Thomond. The official act of renunciation, was performed in the Cathedral of Limerick, after High Mass on 10 July 1558. This act really brought home to the rest of the chiefs the significance of their new position. No longer would they have power over their own lands and people. Instead all things would be ruled by an agent of the English monarch — the Earl of Thomond.

There were, of course, instant rebellions. Most prominent of the dissenters in Thomond were Donogh of Inchiquin and Teigue, who called for assistance from his kinsman, the Earl of Desmond. Conor laid siege on Donogh's castle at Inchiquin. Before he could make any impression on the fortress, the siege was lifted by the arrival of the Earl of Desmond with his army. Conor withdrew to Clanrickard, where he received assistance from the Earl there. Both forces met in a tough struggle at Spancilhill from which the Earls of Thomond and Clanrickard suffered defeat. Many of the O'Briens and MacNamaras fell at the battle of Spancilhill, which was fought in June of 1559. Thus, Donogh and Teigue were restored to Inchiquin and their other possessions.

Conor had to content himself with some raids outside Thomond for the time being. Later, he hurried back when he learned that Donal who had fled to Fermanagh in 1558, had returned. On his arrival Donal was supported by the brothers Teigue and Donogh in raids about the county. Their most notorious effort was an attack on the castle of Rossroe in Clancuilean (Sixmile-bridge), where the Earl happened to be staying at the time. The town nearby, was looted and burned and one hundred of the Earl's men were killed. A great outcry of disgust arose from every corner of West Thomond, so much so that the enemies of the Earl were pursued on all sides. They escaped over the Fergus and afterwards had to employ mercenaries from Clan Sheehy and Clan Sweeney, to help them withstand the pressure from their fellow clansmen. When the Earl of Thomond, with the assistance of English artillery, bombarded and levelled the castle of the Ballyalla, the county was divided between the two forces. The Earl held Ennis and the lands to the east as far as the Shannon; meanwhile Donal and Teigue (Murrogh's sons) on the other side, held West Clare.

Turlogh O'Brien, who was the Bishop of Killaloe at that time, was not leading an exemplary life either. Merchants in Galway went on record to complain that 'on the borders of Thomond, certain outlaws, being bastards of the Bishop of Killaloe, robbed all travellers.' So when he died in 1569, the English were delighted to receive a request from Mac O'Brien of Ara, to have his son appointed to the bishopric. The petition was granted with letters patent and writs issued, and it was the first attempt by the English to install a Protestant bishop in West Thomond. They also thought it opportune to have a public display of their new found authority in the district. With this in mind, Sir Edward Fitton, President of Connaught, (Thomond was attached to Connaught at that time) proclaimed that an assizes was to be held in Ennis, in February 1570.

Teigue O'Brien, a son of Murrogh of Inchiquin, the first sheriff of Clare, arranged for the hearing to be held in the Franciscan Monastery of Ennis. The court went into session without Conor, Earl of Thomond, making an appearance, much to the consternation of Sir Edward. A cavalry detachment was sent to his castle at Clare (Clarecastle), two miles away, on the third day of the sessions. After they had entered the courtyard, they found that the gates had been closed behind them. They were retained as prisoners and many of those outside were killed before they could escape. Fitton left in haste for Galway, with the Earl in hot pursuit. Only for the fact that the English contingent reached Gort castle, they might also have forfeited their lives at the hands of the quarrelsome Earl.

Not at all pleased with his conduct, the English decided to chastise Conor for these outrages. A large army, led by the Earl of Ormond, was sent into West Thomond in an attempt to bring O'Brien to submission. Because both Earls were related, they decided to parley first. The result of it was, that O'Brien gave up all his castles without as much as raising his sword. He then went into exile in France, and Ormond completely subjected the territory to English allegiance. But Conor was not done yet, as we find him the following year in the court of Elizabeth of England begging her pardon. Her Majesty was happy to re-install Conor to his Earldom and he returned in 1571 with a more favourable outlook towards the Crown. When Fitton came down from Connaught a year later to hold his assizes, it was notable that Conor was most helpful to him.

In order to give a snapshot of the period, the following extract is taken from Frost's *History of Clare*:—

QUARRELS OF THE O'BRIENS

In 1573, for some reason not known to us, a war broke out between the O'Briens themselves. It is needless to say that the quarrel was taken up by their partisans on all sides, and that a general plunder of the country was the consequence. What the dispute was about is of very little importance, but in their description of the fighting, the Four Masters give the names of several places in the county, according to their original spelling, which we here reproduce as illustrative of its topography. One of the belligerent parties assembled at Ard-na-Cabóg, near Clare Castle. Thence they marched through Dromcliff, Kilnamona, and Dysert, and 'over the sone road of Coradh-Finne (Corofin), by the gate of the Castle of Inchiquin, and by

Franciscan Friary of Ennis. Founded by the O'Briens in the thirteenth century. South transept and central tower added in the fifteenth century.

Bothar-na-mac Riogh' (the road from Corofin to Killinaboy, called the road of the king's sons, for some reason with which we are unacquainted). They despoiled the church of Cill-inghine-Boaith (Killinaboy), and proceeded in a north-westerly direction, by the confines of Corcomroe and Burren; spreading themselves about, they plundered the country in all directions. Their opponents mustered their forces at Carn-mic-Tail, now Carn-Connachtach, but they had to retire from that place early next morning, their invaders approaching by Slaibh-na-ngroigheadh, keeping Bél-atha-an Ghobhain (Smithstown), on their left. Both armies — one in pursuit of the other, then marched by Cill Mainchin to Bél-an-chip. There a skirmish took place, and one party retreating before their antagonists, by way of Beann Formaile, both arrived at Caherush (Cathair Ruis).

ANOTHER ASSIZES AT ENNIS

Having in view the final subjugation of the Irish of Munster, the Lord Deputy, Sir Henry Sidney, made a progress through that province in 1576. He abolished the ancient customs of 'Coigny, Kernetty, and Bonaght', and ordered that the rules of English law should be substituted for them. He made Donald O'Brien of Ennistymon Governor of the County of Clare, and the new ruler signalised his accession to the office by hanging refractory rebels and malefactors. In this year, Thomond was separated from Connaught and joined to Munster, at the solicitation of the Earl of Thomond. In the following year, Sir William Drury, who had been recently appointed President of Munster, and who had, at Limerick, hanged several of the gentlemen and common people of the O'Briens, held an assizes at Ennis which lasted for eight days. He left the county, after he had appointed a marshal to compel the inhabitants to pay tribute of ten pounds for each barony to the Queen, an impost wholly unknown to the Dal gCais up to that time. The lands of the Earl of Thomond were not exempted from payment, although he had proceeded to England to obtain that favour, as well as to complain of the injury and injustice done to him by his kinsmen. His journey, however, was not quite unproductive of advantage. He obtained from Elizabeth a renewed grant of all his lands, pardon for his people, and a patent conveying to him most of the Church lands and livings of the county. He did not long survive his return home, for his death occurred in 1580, his age being forty-five years, during twenty-two of which he enjoyed the chieftainship of his race. He was buried in the abbey of Ennis, and his eldest son Donogh succeeded, as fourth Earl of Thomond.

The new Earl had been educated in England. Not surprisingly he proved to be very pro-English in his activities. Both he and his father, Conor, had deviated completely from the spirit of the clans. They had become great agents for the English, but very poor Irishmen.

At this time a firm decision was made on a capital town for Clare. The English Queen instructed the president of Connaught to divide the county into baronies and nominate a capital town. Clarecastle would have been selected as the most suitable spot, but the Earl of Thomond insisted on keeping it for himself. Ennis was chosen because it had become prominent when the assizes were held in the monastery. The entire county was then divided up into the present known baronies.

An incident occurred about that time which warrants special mention. One of those who took part in the Clanrickard rebellion, Donogh Beg O'Brien, fell into the hands of the Sheriff of Clare. Cruise, the sheriff, delivered Donogh Beg to the new Lord Deputy, Sir John Perrot, who was in Quin receiving submissions from the other insurgents. As an example of this justice, he first half hanged Donogh Beg O'Brien from the shafts of a car. His entire body was then crushed and mangled by blows from a heavy axe. Most of his bones were broken. Next, his battered and bleeding body was carried to the tower of Quin Abbey, and was fastened there with ropes. It was to be a feast for the birds of the air.

Around the end of the sixteenth century, administration in Clare underwent a great change. It commenced being governed like an English county and was, in fact, henceforth known as County Clare. An end had been put to the two thousand year old system of Brehon law of succession. This, and the clan ownershp of land, had been prime retarders of material progress in the county. For who would farm extensively only to have his crops destroyed by marauders? Who would build a fine house only to have it burned to the ground by raiding clans?

The Irish chiefs and fighting men were not beaten by a lack of courage, but by superior organisation. In the forthcoming centuries, they were still to suffer for their inability to provide a superior system for governing their country.

Chapter 7

English Rule
(1580 — 1640)

The Lord Deputy, Sir John Perrot, convened a parliament in Dublin on 26 April 1585. The outcome of this meeting was that the country would be governed more in keeping with the English administrative system, rather than the haphazard Irish method which was in use until that time. As a result of this, the Governor of Connaught and Clare, Sir Richard Bingham, imposed new taxes in his district. A levy of ten shillings had to be paid yearly for every quarter of one hundred and twenty acres. This was payable to Her Majesty's Government and it was sanctioned by the nobility of Clare on 17 August 1585. The following is an extract taken from the agreement:

Indenture, dated the 17th of August 1585, between Sir John Perrot, knight, of the one part, and the Lords spiritual and temporal, chieftains, gentleman, etc., of that part of the province of Connaught called Thomond, that is to say, Donogh Earl of Thomond; Murrogh Baron of Inchiquin; the Reverend Fathers in God, Mauritius (Murtagh O'Brien Ara), Bishop of Killaloe, Daniel, Elect-Bishop of Kilfenora, (Daniel O'Griffy, Vicar-General); Donogh O'Horan, Dean of Killaloe; Daniel O'Shanny, Dean of Kilfenora; Denis Archdeacon of the same; Sir Edward Waterhouse of Doonass, knight; Sir Turlogh O'Brien of Ennistymon, knight; John MacNamara (Finn) of Knappogue, otherwise called MacNamara of West Clan Culein; Donald Reagh Mac-Namara of Garruragh, otherwise called MacNamara of East Clan Culein; Teige Mac Mahon of Clonderlaw, otherwise called MacMahon of Corcabaskin East; Turlogh MacMahon of Moyarta, chief of his name in Corcabaskin West; Murtagh O'Brien of Dromline, (brother of the Earl of Thomond); Mahone O'Brien of Cloondovan, gent.; Owny O'Loghlen of Greggans, otherwise called the O'Loghlen; Ross O'Loghlen of Glencolumbkille, Tanist to the same O'Loghlen; Mahone and Dermot O'Dea of Cragbrien, chief of his name; Turlogh, son of Teigue O'Brien of Ballycorick, gent.; Luke Brady, son and heir to the late bishop of Meath; Edward White of Cratloe, gent.; George Cusack of Dromoland, gent.; Boetius Clancy of Knockfinn, gent.; John MacNamara of Mountallon, gent.; Henry O'Grady of the Island of Inchicronan, gent.; Donogh MacClancy of the Urlan, chief of his name; Donogh Garv O'Brien of Ballycessy, gent.; Conor O'Brien of Cahircorcran, gent.; and George Fanning of Limerick, merchant, of the other part.

Witnesseth, that all Irish titles shall be abolished; the inhabitants are to grant to the Queen ten shillings a-year for every quarter of land containing one hundred and twenty acres that bears either horn or corn, in lieu of all other demands, save

Typical well fortified tower house of the period.
(Actual picture of present day Dunguaire Castle on the Clare/Galway border).

the raising of horse and foot for her Majesty. The Earl of Thomond is to surrender all claims upon Inchiquin in favour of Baron Inchiquin, but he is to have five shillings per quarter of annual rent out of Clonderlaw, Moyarta, Burren, and part of Tulla, except such lands as belong to the See of Killaloe. Out of other parts of Tulla, Lord Inchiquin is to be paid a yearly rent of five shillings for each quarter, the bishop of Killaloe's lands to be exempted; and out of Corcomroe, he is to receive five shillings per quarter, but his claim is not to extend to the denominations owned by the bishop and dean of Kilfenora, nor to the property of Boetius Clancy, 'in consideration of his birth, learning and good bringing up'; nor to that of Sir Turlogh O'Brien of Ennistymon.

There were twenty prominent signatures to the document which enforced this new system of land tenure. But significantly, the powerful MacNamaras flatly refused to have anything to do with it. In addition to the ten shillings, it was also required of the landowners that they provide forty horsemen and two hundred footmen for the service of the Crown, when required.

To ensure that things would go smoothly, the English showed generosity towards the Earl of Thomond. He was entitled to five shillings rent for every quarter of land in his possession. Most of the Church lands belonging to the various abbeys had been confiscated (like the sixteen and a half quarters in Corcomroe under the Bishop of Kilfenora). This extra land was used by the English to bribe the Irish nobility. The Earl received large tracts of land in the Baronies of Islands and Bunratty, and all of Ibricken. Inchiquin and Tulla baronies were bestowed on the Baron of Inchiquin. The Bishop of Killaloe received five quarters around his house in Killaloe, while the Bishop of Kilfen-ora was presented with four quarters adjoining his house in the parish. An attempt to grant lands was made to the MacNamaras. But the English had to acknowledge in the grant, that the MacNamaras had challenged their right to do so. Provision for this claim had to be inserted in the wording of the document. Two others of note to come into special favour were Dr James Neylon of Ennis, and Boetius Clancy of Knockfinn. Most people in possession of castles and small parcels of lands were made official grants of them by the Crown.

Other than the main MacNamara clans, the only other resistance offered to the English impositions was the lone stand made by Mahon O'Brien at his castle of Cloon Dovan. He was a brave man of resolute character, who saw the tenureship of Irish land for what it was — English takeover. Bingham came down from Connaught with a strong military force carrying firearms and cannon When he arrived at Cloon Dovan in Kilkeady, six miles north-east of the village of Corofin, he found the strong stone castle well fortified and prepared for siege. With cannon and military hardware, Bingham assaulted the ramparts. He quickly realised that it would be difficult to take it. Such was the strength of the structure, that the cannon balls did little more than rebound from the limestone walls. Bingham spent three fruitless weeks at its gates with no success in sight. Finally he placed sharpshooters all around the fortress. They were positioned to cover every conceivable angle, thereby mak-

Knappoque Castle.

ing it difficult for the defenders to safely engage in their activities of flinging out missiles. It was such a sharpshooter that mortally wounded Mahon O'Brien on the battlements of his castle. In panic, the rest of the defenders surrendered. This was their error though, for the cruel Sir Richard Bingham never took prisoners. All the defenders were callously put to the sword. The English forces demolished the castle as much as they could. Only one bare wall marks the location today.

There were many other smaller acts of revolt about the county around that time. The English were so intent on maintaining some measure of rule, that they hanged approximately seventy men and women in Ennis. They found it necessary to establish a jail there (1591) and appointed Patrick Morgan as jailer. This act clearly emphasised their authority in Clare for the first time.

The remains of the disastrous Spanish Armada were, at that time, foundering off the Clare coast. In September of 1588 seven ships sheltered in the Shannon estuary, near Carrigaholt. The Coroner for Thomond, Nicholas Cahane, boarded one of the ships. He could not understand Spanish, but he did learn that they badly needed water. To procure this commodity the Spanish sent a longboat to Kilrush with an offer to exchange a barrel of wine for every barrel of water supplied. However, Sir Richard Bingham had warned the people not to assist the Spanish, so the offer was refused. After refitting on Scattery Island, the ships moved into the open sea and turned south for their homeland.

A day later another vessel was seen at anchor off Liscannor. The purser whose name was Pedro Baptista, came ashore, explaining that the master of the ship and some men had already died of thirst. A vessel was wrecked just off Doonbeg with about three hundred men going down with her. A small number struggled to the beach where many of them were killed by the natives. One of the large vessels went aground between Mutton Island and the shoreline, resulting in the death of a thousand more men. The wreckage was the scene of much plunder for many days, with the natives from all over converging on the disaster area. All that remains of her is a large table which can still be seen in Bunratty castle. The Spaniards who managed to get ashore without being harmed by the natives were taken into custody by the high sheriff, Boetius Clancy, and executed.

The Earl of Thomond was by this time committed to the English cause. When Bingham needed assistance to quell the riotous Burkes in Connaught, he called on Thomond to assist him. This the Earl did in 1593, 1596 and 1597.

After a sojourn in England we next find the Earl and the Baron of Inchiquin joining forces with the English against Hugh O'Donnell. There was an outright revolt in the north of Ireland at the time. While crossing the river Erne they were attacked by O'Donnell's forces. Inchiquin was struck by a bullet which entered his coat of mail through an opening under his arm. He died immediately from his wound and was buried in the abbey of Assaroe. Their campaign against O'Donnell was not very successful. After a short spell in the field they were obliged to retreat back across the Erne, leaving some valuable artillery pieces behind them.

Red Hugh O'Donnell was not at all pleased with the Earl of Thomond for joining with the English in battle against him. He led an army down to

Thomond in 1599 to obtain some measure of retribution. When the northern army arrived at the Clare border, O'Donnell split his forces into three sections. One group went into the Burren to plunder it. Another detachment raided around Ballyogan, Cailmore, Tullyodea and as far as Ballygriffey. The main force marched into Rockforest and Kilnaboy. They gathered much spoils and eventually all raiding parties regrouped and departed northwards out of the county through the territory of Clanrickard. No doubt, token resistance was offered by individuals, but no organised defence was evident in the county.

Seemingly, O'Donnell was not happy that he had done enough to convince the Claremen of his hatred for allies of the English. For the following year (1600), he returned to the county to engage in more plunder. His army entered the county near Moyroe and Tuamgraney. Next, he stopped off at Ennis, from which he sent out raiding parties all over the county. Many houses were burned and crops destroyed. A day later he marched northwards and camped overnight in Clarinbridge in Galway, before returning to his home country.

Soon there was open conflict in the county between those who supported the English religion, land tenure and language, and those who did not. The nobility in Clare were by then speaking English but the majority of ordinary people still conversed in Gaelic. Under James of England, the Earl of Thomond was expected to enforce laws and impose fines to compel Catholics into attending Protestant services. They were also obliged to cut their long hair to make them resemble the English style. Even the mode of dress was dictated by the English.

Religious persecution took place on a large scale. While the Protestant bishop O'Brien was able to collect his tithes only with assistance of the Earl, his counterpart, the Catholic bishop O'Mulryan, did not feel safe in living within the county. Such was the severity of the victimisation that a group of priests requested a ship, to leave the country altogether. One was provided at Scattery Island where forty-six religious boarded her. When the ship was well out to sea all Catholics aboard were reputedly thrown overboard.

When the Catholic priests were driven out, the churches began to fall into ruin. It was about then that many of the fine old religious structures were rendered roofless and useless. The Protestant ministers who officiated had a very small congregation to administer to, since the natives did not take up the new doctrine to any great extent.

The end of the sixteenth century and much of the early part of the seventeenth century saw many inquisitions held at Ennis, Sixmilebridge and other population centres throughout the county. These hearings were primarily concerned with the transferring of inheritances when land owners died. Records of all these numerous transactions were written in Latin and have been kept in the Irish Records Office in Dublin. The real purpose of the hearings was, of course, to establish clearly ownership of property so that appropriate taxes could be levied.

Many of the Ennis sittings were held before local juries and with the following chairmen often presiding:— Nicholas Kenny; Sir John Denham (Knight); John, Bishop of Kilfenora; John Evans and the durable Boetius Clancy. Invariably, the Ennis proceedings were held in the Franciscan Abbey, the ruined structure of which still stands in the street of the same name.

An entry of inquisitions fairly typical of the times reads as follows:-

Inquisition, taken at Ennis, on 19 March 1619, finds that Donogh Grana (the Nasty) O'Brien, late of Mogowna, died on 22 December 1612, being owner of Ardcarney, of three bedrooms in the castle of Magowna, to wit the 'white chamber', the 'guard chamber', and one other near the court; of the land of Inchicolaght, Drumboige, and Deeroolagh; finds that he held these lands from Dermot, Baron of Inchiquin, finds that Syra is the widow, and that Conor is the son and heir of said Donogh, finds that the lands of Teeronaun are now in the possession of Sir Roger O'Shaughnessy in his capacity of Guardian of William Neylon (his stepson); finds that Brian NaMocoiree (the early riser) O'Brien, had conveyed the lands of Ardcarney to Turlogh NaMocoiree, by deed of 1616; finds that Marcus O'Griffy and his wife enjoyed the produce of this land, and that the fee simple was claimed, as his right by James, son of Nicholas Neylon.

Only occasional individual resistance was offered in the county to the complete takeover by the Crown. Organisation like theirs was completely new and bewildering to the native Irish. With the principal clan leaders, the O'Briens, acting as English Earls, leadership and a lack of direction was missing. It was no surprise therefore that a united Irish front was not presented to the alien domination. By the time that the 4th Earl, Donogh, died in 1624 and his son Henry became the 5th Earl they had contributed much to English plantation and to the fostering of Protestantism. Because they received much of their education in England and spent a good deal of their time there, they were (not surprisingly) very English in outlook. Yet this did not prevent Henry's

Clare divided into baronies by the English, 1579.

brother, Barnabas, from being extremely discontented with English recognition of the O'Brien family claims.

When the English monarchy passed from the Catholic James to the Protestant Charles I in 1625, Ireland was not as well settled constitutionally as he would like it. He therefore encouraged his agents in Ireland to proceed with the plantation of Clare in whatever way they could. In a letter from Whitehall to the Lord Deputy in Ireland in 1637, instructions were given 'to go on with the plantation in the county of Clare, and from His Majesty you may expect encouragement and support'.

So down-trodden were the people, that in the year 1640 it was recorded in a Parliament convened in Dublin that 'the many grievous, exactions, pressures and vesicatious proceedings of some of the clergy of this kingdom, and their officers and ministers, against the laity, especially the poorer sort, to the great impoverishment and general detriment of the whole kingdom'. Conditions were bad in Clare but they were worse in some other counties. Little surprise therefore, to find rebellion in the north quickly spreading to Clare.

Chapter 8

Rebellion and Oppression (1641 — 1800)

It was not totally unexpected when a bitter revolt broke out in Ulster in 1641. The province had been heavily planted with impoverished settlers from Scotland. News of the rebellion was first received in Clare at the great fair of Quin. It was enthusiastically adopted in the county as a signal to strike a blow against all English settlers.

Because the English gentry had secured themselves in most of the Irish castles, it was logical that attacks would be made on these fortresses. Ballyalla Castle, situated near Ennis, was the first to be put to the test. All Protestants of Ennis and its vicinity had fled there for safety.

In a prelude to storming the castles, many native leaders drove off the stock belonging to the English farmers. The Earl of Thomond, Barnabas, judged that the culprits should be hanged. Most other leaders did not agree, and put up bail for the accused. For two unfortunates who could not arrange bail, their fate was hanging from the battlements of Bunratty Castle.

About 9 December 1641 a fairly interesting case came to light. Oliver and John Delahoyde of Fomerla, drove away the herds of John Ivisden, Thomas Pandell and those of many other English planters. This angered the Earl, so he sent mounted and foot troops to arrest the brothers. John was found to be dying, but Oliver was brought before his Lordship. With oaths and tears he swore to the Earl that he was innocent of the charges. Falling for this dramatic plea, Barnabas released him. Barnabas further empowered him with martial law to apprehend any offenders he might find in his own district. Delahoyde was not long returned to his home country when he resumed his old activities of driving off English cattle!

When many of the poorer English settlers had gained admission to Ballyalla Castle it was found that provisions there were not adequate. Initially, some women who were sent out to collect eggs, geese, lambs etc., were waylaid on their return to the keep. They were attacked and beaten, and had their goods taken from them. The attackers warned them if they were caught again, they would be hanged. This preventative action by the rebels halted further relief from entering the castle. Those inside were therefore forced to make do with what was already gathered within.

By 4 February 1642, Captain Dermot O'Brien and other Clare notables had raised an army of about a thousand men from south Connaught and Thomond. He sent a letter to the Cuffes, who were responsible members

Leamenagh Castle home of the O'Brien clan. One of its most famous residents, Máire Rua, who was the wife of Conor O'Brien, lived here in the seventeenth century.

inside the castle (it was Maurice Cuffe, merchant of Ennis, who wrote down all that happened during the siege of Ballyalla). In the letter, O'Brien threatened to storm the castle if they did not wilfully surrender. The Cuffes replied that they would hold the castle for His Majesty's use until their lease expired.

Dermot at once instructed Turlogh O'Brien, the first prominent rebel in the county, to lay siege on the fortress at Ballyalla. The stronghold was surrounded, with groups from each barony taking their turn to keep watch outside. Because the weather was quite cold at that time, the men built huts in the hedgerows in order to keep warm. Meanwhile, one of the MacNamaras went to the north to get a cannon which would be suitable for bombarding the walls. At times, those inside the walls would steal outside and surprise the besiegers. They often managed to grab the temporary wooden roofings, and returned safely with them to be used for firing in the castle. Presently, Mac-Namara returned from the north declaring that it was not possible to acquire a cannon. They were then resigned to settle for a protracted siege.

Besides Turlogh and Dermot O'Brien, there were many more O'Briens in the rebel grouping. They included Sir Daniel O'Brien, Knight of Carrigaholt; Daniel of Carrowduff; Conor, eldest son of Sir Daniel; Conor of Leamenagh and many more of the old clan. Naturally, the MacNamaras were there in great numbers. Very noticeable also in the struggle were the O'Gradys and the O'Shaughnessys. Flann and David Neylon of Rosslevan and Andrew Burke of

Ennis, and numerous others from far and near supported the cause.

On 6 February, safe conduct was offered to those inside Ballyalla if they would surrender. They refused. Therafter, they were verbally abused with threats and oaths from the attackers. The soldiers outside warned them that Turlogh O'Brien had in mind using some instrument on the castle that would leave them no option but to surrender.

Turlogh may have been an admirer of progressive warfare, for he built a leather cannon which was supposed to launch a keg of powder at the walls. Instead it blew out the breach. This caused Turlogh to turn in dubiety to his second device — it was merely a large wooden frame with a pitched roof. The structure was covered with many layers of hides which were designed to withstand musket ball or steel arrrow. The 'sow' as it was called, was rolled to the walls with a number of men safely inside the framework. With this protective canopy over the men, they were able to attack the walls with picks and crowbars. It was a slow business but it did have some effect. Those inside the castle ran short of water and had to venture out in search of some. The raiding party killed a number of men guarding the 'sow' and captured many useful tools and firearms. This success took the sting from the attackers thrusts, and finally the siege petered out, on 12 March. Throughout the year of 1642 the principal activities included the attempted taking of castles by the Irish rebels. In that year cattle rustling was also common. The Irish drove off most of the Englishmen's stock which, after a time, left them very short of food. They therefore were obliged to strike out in raiding parties to take back what they had lost. The defenders of Ballyalla also sallied out to recover cattle and even engaged the rebels in some skirmishes.

Once again, forces led by Donal O'Brien of Leamenagh and Teigue Roe O'Brien besieged Ballyalla. They successfully prevented supplies from getting to the castle and finally the garrison had to surrender for lack of provisions towards the end of September. A noteworthy fact was that those who defended the castle were not harmed after the surrender. Meanwhile, a band of O'Gradys and O'Shaughnessys successfully laid siege to the castle of Inchicronan.

The end of 1642 saw all the English settlers making claims or depositions to the Crown for property lost. It was interesting to note that either the claims were somewhat exaggerated or that the English had become very rich indeed in their new land. James Vandelure, a Dutch Protestant, made a claim for £1,836, naming many of the Irish rebels who owed him money. He lost his house and mills, some outhouses, and four quarters of land.

William Chambers, who lived in Kilrush, claimed that his losses amounted to £1,519. He swore that he was robbed of his cattle, goods and chattels. Ann Asher of Killimer made a deposition for £994, claiming that the O'Cahanes were the culprits. Perhaps the greatest loss of all was that of Gregory Hickman, a British Protestant of Barntick. His deprivations came to £3,672 in cattle, sheep, horses and furniture. He named many who were debtors to him, including Laurence Rice and another Ennis merchant, who allegedly ran off with eighteen packs of his wool. While he was complaining, he took the opportunity to name some Protestants who had turned Papist, and had been seen going to Mass.

The following account from Frost's *History of Clare,* gives an indication of the events of the time:

Edmond O'Flaherty of Connemara came, in April 1642 with a fleet of boats to the coast of Clare, having for his object the expulsion of Peter Ward, an Englishman, from the castle of Tromroe near Miltown-Malbay. He was joined by the following, viz:— Donogh O'Brien of Newtown; Turlogh, Conor, and Mahone, sons of Dermot O'Brien of Tromroe; Richard Fitz Patrick, Seneschal and Receiver of the Earl of Thomond in the barony of Ibricken; Hugh McCurtin; Daniel, son of Scanlane Mac-Gorman; Teige Fitz Patrick of Fintrabeg; Teige Roe O'Brien, son of Sir Daniel O'Brien; Mahone and Donogh McEncarriga of Cloghaneinshy and Fanore; James and Teige, sons of Donald Mergagh Gallery of Poulawillin; Daniel and Mahone Mac-Gorman of Cahermurphy; Hugh Hogan of Ballyhehan; Edmond Oge O'Hogan of Moyhill; Dermot MacGorman of Knockanalban; Gillabreeda MacBrody of Knockanalban; and Loghlen MacCahane of Doonbeg. They laid siege to the castle, and in a few days compelled the garrison to surrender. In the progress of the contest, Peter Ward, his wife Alison, and his son George, were killed. Their bodies were removed for burial to the grave-yard of Kilmurry by order of Daniel O'Brien of Dough, but they were disinterred by direction of Daniel, son of Scanlane Mac Gorman of Drumsallagh, 'a mass priest', and again buried outside the churchyard, for the reason that no heretical corpse of a Protestant should be allowed to repose in consecrated ground. All this is stated in the Deposition of John Ward, son of Peter, who swears that his father's property, worth £871 was plundered. The younger Ward then repaired to Bunratty, to complain to the Earl of Thomond, whose tenant his father had been, that in the act of spoliation, the Earl's confidential agent, Richard Fitz Patrick had been a prime mover. All the redress he got was a cell in the prison of the castle. Having expostulated with the Earl on the hardship of this treatment, he was threatened with a box on the ear. He goes on to declare that, at Newmarket-on-Fergus, he met Teige Roe, son of Sir Daniel O'Brien. That young gentleman, in presence of Cormack Hickey, of Bunratty, surgeon, and of several others, imprecated the curse of God upon any one who did not join the rebellion. He mentions that, after the surrender of the castle of Limerick, on 23 June 1642, part of the garrison repaired to Bunratty to offer their services to the Earl, and that they were refused. He intimates that, with the connivance of the Earl, a brass gun was sent from Limerick, by water, to Clare, and that the piece of ordnance in question was mainly instrumental in capturing that castle as well as Ballyalla. Nothing was easier than to intercept this gun, seeing that a Dutch ship, well armed and laden with rape seed from Limerick to London, then lay in the Shannon, and might have been used for that purpose. Ward was present one day, when the Earl exclaimed to Dermot O'Brien, 'By the Lord of Heaven, Cousin Dermot, if I be not paid my rents, I will retake the castle of Clare, in despite of all your forces. I shall bring Forbes' ships to the place'. Another day, he said to John MacNamara, that his countrymen did mightily slight him in not paying his rents. 'By G— were it not for me Lord Forbes would have spoiled the whole country, and I am nothing the better for it, and nothing the nearer to receive my rents'. His Lordship entertained at Bunratty, with eating and drinking, the most notorious rebels of the county, every one being freely welcome. Ward adds, that Matthew Hicks, who held the castle of Tuamgraney, surrendered it on quarter, and on his way to Bunratty would have been robbed, only for the intervention of the English garrison at Cappagh, near Sixmilebridge.

One of the little Protestant garrisons founded by the Earl of Thomond was situated at Doonass, then called Annaghmore and Annaghbeg. Several of the Clare Depositions have reference to the expulsion of these people by the Irish gentry of the surrounding country. They were, for the most part, small farmers or mechanics, and their names were Roundtree, Pitch, Norman, Cobb, Drury, Capel, Wilkinson, Meale, Culliver, Brine, Derby, Church, and Edwards. Inspired by terror, some members of the colony turned Catholics; among these were, French and Roane of Coollisteigue, and Handcock and Dyer of Doonass. Those who drove them out were Lord Brittas, John M'Namara of Neadanura (Newtown), Geoffrey Burke of Errinagh, and the MacNamaras of Cragleigh.

Every Protestant settler in Clare was either attacked or had his lands and good stolen. Some turned to the Catholic religion to avoid being molested. Most of them eventually retreated to the Protestant held castles of Bunratty (the Earl reluctantly received them) and Limerick.

The Anglo-Irish, who were Catholics, sided with the native Irish. From this allegiance came the Confederation of Kilkenny, at which Lord Mount-Garrett was chosen as president. An army was organised all over Ireland and General Barry was elected supreme commander in Munster. Sir Daniel O'Brien, an uncle of the Earl of Thomond, was given command in Clare. The Protestants began looking to England for assistance. General Barry and Lord Muskerry took Limerick and its castles as a preliminary step. With the exception of Bunratty castle the whole of Clare was now in the hands of the Confederate Catholics. The Parliamentarians, or Protestants, had strongly entrenched themselves at Bunratty and would not be easily removed.

To further strengthen their position at Bunratty, a fleet of ships with supplies and troops was sent from England into the Shannon estuary. The fleet was commanded by Sir William Penn, father of William Penn, who was the founder of Pennsylvania. The ships entered the estuary on 11 March 1646. As they eased their way up towards Bunratty they took time off to molest the inhabitants along the banks. Seven hundred men were landed on an island adjacent to the castle. Meanwhile, negotiations took place between the Earl and a Captain Huntly. The talks finally resulted in the cautious Earl agreeing to allow the Parliamentarians to occupy the fortress. Wisely, the fleet stayed in the estuary and was an added insurance for those defending the castle. Additionally, the men-of-war blocked trade between the confederate held city of Limerick, and the open sea.

This new development troubled the commanders in Limerick city. In order to reassert their position it was necessary to take the castle at Bunratty. They knew that the garrison consisted of about 800 foot and 60 horse, and some cannon. It was under the command of a very able Lt Colonel MacAdam. To further strengthen the place, MacAdam erected earthen fortifications on the north and west perimeters. These were the only sides not afforded the natural protection of the river.

Lord Muskerry rode into Clare leading an army of 3,000 foot and 300 men on horseback. He had very experienced field officers in General Purcell, General Stephenson and Colonel Purcell, all of whom had served in the German wars. Soon after arrival at Bunratty the Confederate soldiers entrenched themselves about the castle. The river Raite (from which the castle takes its name) protected the fortress on the east and south prospects. The Irish, therefore, concentrated their efforts at the north-western side. No great impression could be made on the massive stone structure, even when two field pieces were put into action. In fact, the besieged were able to charge out to engage the Catholics in skirmishes, and these with some successes. When Cardinal Rinuncini arrived from Rome with aid, the Confederates gained great heart. Amongst a large store of supplies, he had with him 20,000 lbs. of powder and six small trunks of Spanish gold. He spent much time in the trenches encouraging the troops and sharing in their dangers. The grounds around Bunratty greatly impressed him. He wrote to his brother in Italy that there was nothing in their country to compare with the palace of Lord Thomond. A vivid description was recorded of the beautiful ponds and parks with its 3,000 head of deer.

A constant fusilade was kept up by the attackers during each day and night. The Parliamentarians became strained by the constant harassment. A fateful break came in the action when a chance shot from a field piece passed through a window and killed Lt Colonel MacAdam. This greatly shook the besieged, so much so that they surrendered shortly afterwards on 13 July 1646. Those that remained of the garrison were allowed to board their ships in the estuary and set sail for Cork. Some of the standards taken from the castle were paraded through Limerick, headed by Rinuncini, to St Mary's Cathedral where a *Te Deum* was sung to celebrate the victory.

The joy was short-lived though, for Lord Inchiquin (Morogh of the Burnings), fighting on the side of the Parliamentarians, commenced to ravage Munster. He slaughtered three thousand persons in Cashel Cathedral, splattering the blood of religious and laity alike, even on the altars. Lord Taafe for the Confederates attempted to intercept him before he reached Cork. Inchiquin's skilled troops, though less in numbers, reduced Taafe's army in half in an engagement near Mallow.

Later, Morogh changed sides and finally died a Catholic in 1674. He was buried, at his own request, in St Mary's Cathedral in Limerick.

If Inchiquin was bad, the Parliamentarians in England still had a complete tyrant to send to Ireland. Cromwell landed in 1649 and ruthlessly slaughtered the southern and eastern fortified towns of the country. Before he could reach Limerick he was recalled to England for more pressing matters. His son-in-law, Ireton, was given command. Ireton's aim was to get into Clare and bring the county under complete control for the Parliamentarians in England. Although Confederate forces under Lorde Castlehaven had fortified the Shannon at Killaloe and O'Briens Bridge, they failed to keep Ireton out of the county. The English managed to ferry troops across the river in spite of the absence of a bridge at O'Briens Bridge. Surprisingly, the Irish retreated without offering resistance. From the north came Ludlow leading more Parliamentarians. He swept through the Burren and North Clare, gathering up much provisions as he went. Finally, he linked with Ireton near Limerick, and they immediately put the city under siege.

There were some English ships in the Shannon river with cannon firepower. A few days previously they had bombarded and taken Carrigaholt. The vessels were next manoeuvred dangerously close to Limerick's walls.

Such was the strength of the English forces at that time, that they could send a detachment of 2,000 foot, 12 horse troops and 8 troops of dragoons under Ludlow, in sweeps all over Clare. They destroyed Carrigaholt, killed a small Irish contingent near Ennis, and slew Conor O'Brien of Leamenagh. Shortly after that Ludlow returned to assist Ireton at Limerick's walls. Meanwhile the Clare forces were standing by at Sixmilebridge. All that they required were instructions from the garrison commander, Hugh O'Neill, in Limerick. Unfortunately, none were received.

There was much desolation in Limerick due to the ravages of a plague. Gradually the defenders lost heart when relief was not forthcoming. Finally on 27 October 1651 the Irish had no other recourse but to surrender.

In a very short time the English forces were establishing themselves in Clare. The castle of Clonroad fell to them and they kept the castle of Clare under constant siege. On 8 September Ireton entered Bunratty. Having seen all the other strongholds fall, Captain William Butler surrendered Clare Castle on the first day of November, 1651.

Clare was ravaged and utterly despoiled by the English under Ludlow. The only harm that the county would inflict on him was the discomforts of its climate, from which he contracted a bout of sweating. It is to him also, that the following is attributed regarding the Burren:— 'It is a country where there is not water enough to drown a man, wood enough to hang one, nor earth enough to bury him, which last is so scarce that the inhabitants steal it from one another.' Ludlow died of his fever, probably pneumonia, in the winter of 1652.

The ten year war had completely reduced the population so that communities were sparse indeed. In June of 1653, out of 1,300 townlands only forty were inhabited, mostly in the Barony of Bunratty. A census revealed that there were only 16,474 Catholics and 440 English Protestants in Clare in 1659. Hundreds were taken to Cork harbour and transported into slavery to the Barbados. By 1680 the population crept back up to 30,000 inhabitants.

It was reported that people fed on dead horses and even their own kind in order to sustain their miserable lives. All churches and castles not held by the English were demolished. Priests were hunted down and dared not show their cloth. An example of the cruelty of Cromwell's soldiers can be seen from the fact that two of his officers, Captains Stace and Asper put five hundred families to death in the baronies of Islands, Ibricken, Clonderlaw and Moyarta.

Where were Clare's leaders during this worst ever disaster to befall the county? Barnabas, the Earl of Thomond, retired to England and died there in 1657. Morogh, whom we referred to earlier, fought some of his best battles for the Parliamentarians against the natives and Anglo-Irish. He would have been better employed protecting his own homeland, no matter what his religion. It was unfortunate for the Irish cause that he did not, for he was a most able general. He had been educated in the best military schools in England, and proved to be a ruthless commander. When he retired to France he was offered high positions in their forces. As was mentioned earlier he finally died a Catholic and donated twenty pounds to the Friars in Ennis to say masses for his soul.

Towards the end of the century Lord Clare's Dragoons, who had been formed from around Carrigaholt, saw much action in the north of the country. However, even they could not help King James storm the city of Derry which was being defended by the Williamites. The Dragoons, as well as James' army, suffered a decisive defeat at the battle of the Boyne in 1690. This was probably the turning point in the war, and the Irish forces, minus King James, retreated west of the Shannon. While Limerick was under siege, Patrick Sarsfield led five hundred men at night through Clare and crossed the Shannon at Killaloe into Tipperary. He was successful in blowing up a supply train of munitions at Ballyneety, and returned as he came, back to Limerick.

During assaults on the walls, a hasty command by a French officer to close a drawbridge at Thomond Gate in the city, resulted in many Irish soldiers being trapped outside on an access bridge. They were slaughtered without quarter, so that bodies were piled five and six deep on the bridge. After six weeks spirits sagged. Supplies became very low. Negotiations were begun on the third day of October and these resulted in the Treaty of Limerick being signed.

As far as Clare was concerned, the surrender of Limerick meant two things. Firstly, nearly all the soldiers, many of them from Clare, decided to emigrate to France and serve with the French forces. Presumably they hoped to have another day against the English, but with the might of the French army behind them. Indeed it was their privilege in that army, that they would be sent to the front lines whenever the enemy was English.

The second effect which the surrender of Limerick had on Clare was that the county became defenceless and wide open for complete English takeover. The wars had left the population extremely thin and poverty and hunger was widespread. The county was without effective Irish leadership, so it was a relatively simple task for the English to establish their authority.

There was much doling out of confiscated lands around 1667 to prominent people. Recipients included Daniel O'Brien (Lord Viscount Clare), the Earl of Inchiquin and the Protestant Bishop of Killaloe. Final settlements were made in the reign of William of Orange.

Because William was a Dutchman, we find a number of Dutch settlers as well as English, obtaining grants of land in the county. A Joost Van Keppel received most of Lord Clare's property near Carrigaholt. Lord Clare had elected to sail for France with the 'Wild Geese'. The Vandeleur family gained much at this time and titles of property have remained in their name down to present times. Some families, which still held land until recent times, purchased their properties for nominal sums at auctions from which Catholics were banned. A couple that come to mind are the levers family and the O'Callaghan-Westropps (property sold to Swiss businessman in the 1970s). In fact all the large estates in Clare were acquired in these settlements under King William, around 1700.

Before leaving the seventeenth century, for the odious conditions which prevailed throughout the eighteenth, it might be enlightening to read a pen picture of Clare's capital — Ennis. Donogh, Earl of Thomond, obtained a grant in 1609 to hold a market on Tuesdays in the town. There were also two fairs, one on Easter Monday and the day after; and the other on 24 and 25 August. Ennis was constituted a borough on 26 September 1612. It was managed by a

CLONROAD CASTLE, 1680.

provost and twelve burgesses. The provost was empowered to make by-laws, he had a mercatory guild and a common seal. He was also clerk to the market, with two sergeants at arms and two inferior officers.

The town traded extensively in hides, tallow and butter, which the buyers transported to Limerick by using the river Fergus. There were about 120 houses in the Ennis of 1680. The population was estimated at 600 inhabitants. Twenty of the houses in the town were slated and the rest were thatched. The principal buildings were the Franciscan Abbey, the Hall of Assizes, Lenthall's Inn, and of course Clonroad Castle. A Denis Casey was town clerk in 1687.

The 1700s blew in the cold harsh Penal Laws to persecute the smitten Irish. There was an estimated population of about sixty thousand in Clare as the century unfolded. Ninety per cent of those lived in the inhuman conditions of slaves. To further aggravate their plight the English laws pounded the bewildered people into deeper subservience. Though the Irish were promised freedom and religious tolerance by the Treaty of Limerick, they saw very little of that.

Laws were passed to 'banish all Papists and regulars of the Popish clergy, out of the kingdom.' Clerics found in the country could be either imprisoned, transported or executed. The Clare members who sat in the Parliament that passed the Penal Laws were, Sir Donogh O'Brien and Sir Henry Ingoldsby. Representing the Borough of Ennis at this same parliament were Francis Gore and Francis Burton.

Laws enticing Catholics to become Protestants were then enacted. For example, if any member of a Catholic family turned to Protestantism, the family's property immediately became his by law. In the event of a Protestant adopting the Catholic religion his belongings fell to the nearest Protestant relative. There were heavy fines for practising clerics and for those who would not disclose the names of priests. A pleasing feature of the times was that a good number of local Protestants were unwilling to enforce many of the rigid laws on their Catholic neighbours. But by the time Queen Ann died in 1714 many oppressive laws had been written into the books.

The greater part of the eighteenth century was taken up with the passing of acts and laws to prevent the growth of Popery. In spite of all the poverty and cruelty, the Catholic numbers steadily increased in Clare.

Much of the countryside was well wooded at this time. Even around the western seaboard, large forests were plentiful. Folklore has it, that when cattle strayed around Tulla and Quin, they would not be very easy to find due to the thickness of the woods there. All the area between Kilkishen, Tulla and Quin was a sea of trees. But gradually most of the fine forests were stripped to supply the lucrative English market. It is said that the majestic oaks around Killaloe were felled to build some of the finest ships in the English navy.

Roads were in the roughest order. Invariably they meandered along the high ground, which was hard enough to take winter traffic. Mode of transporation was little less than primitive. Goods were carried to market on pack horses, or even on crude sleighs pulled by these animals. The farmer and his wife would ride to town on horseback — if they owned a horse. Most walked.

This state of affairs made the horse a much sought after commodity. The breeding of these animals became more lucrative. To display and sell the horses, such gatherings as the fair of Spancilhill were initiated. Indeed fairs and markets were the only remaining places where people could eject themselves from the misery of their surroundings.

Coming to the end of the eighteenth century we find that the oppressive laws were not being too rigidly enforced anymore. Some priests were even allowed to build small thatched roofed churches, provided that they were not too ostentatious. Feelings gradually improved between both communities, although it must be said that Clare did not have the worst landowners. Many of them had Irish blood running through their veins and were therefore somewhat more easily disposed towards their Catholic neighbours.

Even parliamentary progress was being made in the country. Sheriff Poole Hickman convened a meeting on 6 April 1782 in Ennis, of gentry, clergy and free-holders. The outcome of it was that they enthusiastically supported the Irish Parliament in their recent resolutions. Essentially those declarations entailed that the Commons of Ireland should have the right to make laws for its own country. They further claimed that for any body of men, other than King, Lords and Commons of Ireland to make laws for the country was unconstitutional. A vote of confidence was given to Clare's representatives in Parliament, namely, Sir Lucius O'Brien and Edward Fitzgerald.

A particular feature of the end of this century was the attempted risings, in other parts of Ireland, of 1782, 1798 and 1800. There was no such rebellions in Clare but the people did experience some of the fringe activities. The English Yeomanry searched about the country looking for any who might sympathise with rebels and United Irishmen. The Yeomanry were a cruel lot, and inflicted instant punishments if they did not get the desired co-operation. Those under suspicion were brought to Limerick for court martial. Whipping,

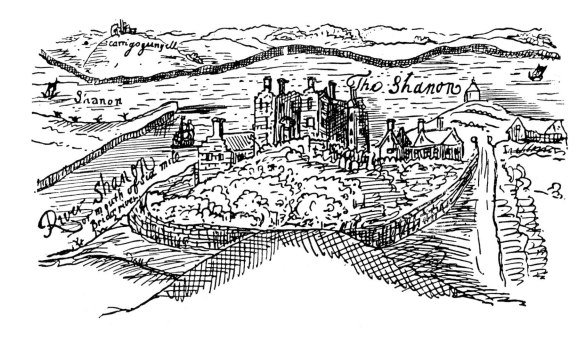

Dineley's sketch of Bunratty Castle in 1680.

transportation and hangings on the bridge, were the usual punishments.

Although times were difficult, a love of learning was evident in the eighteenth century. The hedge schools were well attended. Those masters in the ditches were often much more than mere teachers, many were literary men of distinction. Some of the poets in Clare were Hugh and Andrew Mac-Curtin, in the early part of the century. The poet James Considine came from Mullagh and Brian Merriman taught school in Feakle, although he was reputedly born in Kilmihil. Irish was the language of the poets already mentioned, but the Ennis man, Thomas Dermody wrote in English. Undoubtedly this man Dermody was a literary genius. He knew Greek and Latin from four years of age, and wrote very good poetry in his tenth year. At eleven he ran away from home and led a varied and unhappy life in Dublin. Dermody was wounded while serving with the British army in Flanders. He died in miserable conditions in London when he was only twenty-seven.

To add to the list of characters of that time, there was MacNamara of Moyreisk. He was very fond of duelling and was quite adept with either pistol or sword. The man from Moyreisk gained for himself and his family the nickname 'Fireball' MacNamara. No direct descendant of his has come down to present times.

In the eighteenth century there were two factors which checked the unleashing of starvation in the country as well as in Clare. The principal diet of the time was potatoes. Many failures of the crop were known in this century:— 1739 the crop was completely destroyed; in 1740 entire failure was reported: 1770 there was failure due to curl; in 1800 it was widespread failure.

The crop was always subject to some disease or another and this was generally accepted.

The unusually low population of about half a million people at the worst stage, and the fact that the Irish Parliament had some say in what went on in the country, were the main items to stave off a disastrous famine. If the population were drastically to increase and the Irish Parliament were not there to influence English opinion, the gateway would be thrown open to starvation and annihilation of the people.

Clare Castle in 1680 from Dineley's Journal. Note similarities with Lawrence photograph on page 98 at the end of chapter nine.

Chapter 9

Famine Years
(1801 — 1900)

The most significant event to occur in the early part of the nineteenth century was undoubtedly the Union of Ireland and Britain. As of the beginning of January 1801, the Irish parliament was abolished. Instead of the greater wealth of England enriching the poorer Ireland, as Pitt put it, the stronger completely drained the weaker.

Catholics were still without freedom of any kind. The 1793 Act had given all forty shilling freeholders the right to vote for Members of Parliament. However, Catholics were not allowed to stand in elections, so that the voters were left with the choice of voting for only a suitable Protestant candidate. Usually what happened was the local landlord instructed his own peasantry as to how they should vote. So, one of the principal objectives to be fought for in this century was Catholic Emancipation.

More in desperation than in hope, the Clare Catholics were following the fortunes of the Napoleonic wars in Europe. Hundreds of Claremen were in the French ranks fighting against the old enemy. Even though many Irishmen had been serving with the British forces, the hearts of the people at home lay with Napoleon. There was a vague expectation that if the French Emperor conquered England, that the Irish Catholic would gain his freedom.

Closer to home the Irish were producing their own emperor and it was not too long before they realised it. A Kerry barrister named Daniel O'Connell fought every Irish law case for the Catholic underdog. He steadily built up the morale of the people by showing them that even the law itself could be beaten at times. His activities awoke in the Irish a sense of injustice by England, which they had not fully appreciated before.

It must be stated though, that the Protestant people of Clare were a fair-minded and humane community. They held a meeting in Ennis in 1807 to demand the liberation of their Catholic neighbours from the yoke of the cruel laws that oppressed them. This was in spite of a Protestant Orange Organisation elsewhere in the country seeking to assert themselves as higher class citizens than Catholics.

Major MacNamara, an officer from Clare, rendered Daniel O'Connell invaluable technical aid when he was challenged to a duel by D'Esterre in 1815. O'Connell won the duel, due mainly to the expert duelling advice received from Major MacNamara. This act of MacNamara's made the people of Clare proud. The fact that one of their own helped to save the life of the great Emancipator ignited a loving attachment between the Clare Catholics and O'Connell.

The year 1822 brought another famine to the county. It is not as renowned as the 1846 and 1847 famines but, no doubt, the hunger and suffering was just as bad. Perhaps not as many potatoes were affected. There were, at least, partial crops here and there. But with the population rapidly increasing each year, it was becoming extremely difficult to feed the people on potatoes alone. The dramatic increase in population is something of a puzzle if one considers the abject poverty. The Catholic bishop of Raphoe may have had an explanation in part when he told the Irish Pool Inquiry of 1835: 'They cannot (the peasants) be worse off than they are ... and they may help each other.' Girls married at sixteen and boys at seventeen or eighteen. Irishwomen were noted as being exceptionally fertile, nineteen in twenty of them having children at least every second year for twelve years.

In 1841 when a census was taken, the population of Ireland had reached 8,175,124, which led Disraeli to declare that Ireland was the most densely populated country in Europe at the time. He asserted that areas in Ireland were more densely populated than parts of China.

It even seems possible that the census figures were very much on the low side. A relief officer wrote that the Census of 1841 was 'pronounced universally to be no fair criterion of the present population'. He had it tested in County Clare and found that the population was one third greater than had been recorded. It can be assumed therefore that when the famine of 1845 came the population might well have been greater than nine million.

This increase in population led to huge problems in living off the land — the only means of sustaining the labourers family. The land was divided and sub-divided, again and again. Holdings were split into smaller and still smaller fragments until families were attempting to exist on plots of less than an acre, in some cases even less than half an acre. As rents were extremely high (at 100% higher than in England) not many could afford to buy or rent large plots. A system of hiring out land, called conacre, evolved.

Conacre was a contract where a portion of land was let to grow crops. It was not a lease but a licence to occupy. The owner was obliged to manure and prepare the ground to receive crops. It was the obligation of the hirer to provide the seed, plant it and harvest it. Rent was very high, between £10 and £14 for good ground while poor ground fetched around £6 an acre. The demand for conacre was overwhelming and without it more people would have starved.

On the political front, the Catholic Association proposed that O'Connell should stand in the election of 1828 as a candidate for Clare. At first, O'Connell was reluctant to run against the Protestant Vesey Fitzgerald, who was a fair man and a good landlord. Eventually, the Kerry barrister was successfully persuaded by his friends to contest the election. From the moment the decision was made, the campaign was organised with considerable zeal.

O'Connell had two dedicated and talented men working for him in the county. Tom Steele, a Protestant and a landowner, did much to pacify and unite the people in the cause of Catholic Emancipation. Steele was a landlord of considerable wealth. His country house overlooked Cullane Lake which lies between Kilkishen and Tulla. The second devotee of O'Connell was The O'Gorman Mahon who was born in Mill Street, Ennis. O'Gorman Mahon led the life of a gentleman, thanks to the amount of property he inherited from his father who was a merchant in the town. Early in life he adopted the suffix 'O'Gorman' from his mother's family into his own name. It was a source of great pride to him and he would not hesitate to challenge those who questioned his right to use it. Being a man given to fighting rather frequently, he would call the disrespectful to a duel without requiring much provocation. One of his favourite weapons was the 'under and over' pistol. He was elected as MP for Ennis in 1847 and 1879.

Most of the voters in Clare were made up of the small farming people in the form of the forty shilling freeholders. It was necessary to woo them away from voting as they traditionally did, i.e. for a Protestant candidate favoured by their landlords. O'Gorman Mahon and Steele were soon doing the rounds of the county to impress upon the freeholders the importance of voting for Daniel O'Connell. The reputations of both Steele and The O'Gorman Mahon as noted duellists, ensured that the landlords did nothing to impede them in their work.

Polling days, for there were two, saw masses of people jammed into the narrow streets of Ennis. The attention of the entire United Kingdom was focused on the little courthouse in the square (where the O'Connell monument now stands) in the centre of town. There were many police and soldiers on duty, but the mood was more festive than unharmonious, and happily their services were not required.

In a pre-election speech the outgoing candidate, Fitzgerald, made a moving and finely balanced address to voters. O'Connell, the great orator that he was, commenced his own delivery with a bout of sarcastic humour which won the hearts of the people to him. He concluded his speech in a thundering voice, laying before the simple Clare peasants what would be in store for them should they fail to elect a Catholic candidate. When he had finished, the people were so taken by his words that Mr Fitzgerald's speech was almost entirely forgotten.

On the first polling day Catholics were asked to produce written evidence that they had taken the Oath of Allegiance. Some confusion resulted from this new tactic by the establishment. Therefore most of the voting on the opening day was registered by the Protestant people. Fortunately, by the second day, Steele and The O'Gorman Mahon had the long lines of Catholic voters well versed in swearing the oath, which ensured that large numbers of them voted. The result, favouring O'Connell by 982 votes, was received with tumultuous jubilation by the people of Clare and Ireland. Clare had achieved an all time first by returning a Catholic MP to Westminster. It gained for the county the deserved title of 'The Banner County', or the leading one. It was in the true spirit of the old Dalcassians of being the first into the fray.

O'Connell went on to fight for Catholic Emancipation and Repeal of the Union of Ireland and Britain. Some small measure of freedom was handed to Catholics in the 1829 Bill. But a severe body blow was delivered in the same

An eviction scene during the Famine (The Illustrated London News Picture Library).

legislation when the forty shilling freeholders were deprived of their right to vote. A very potent weapon had been nipped in the bud by the astute English politicians. Henceforth a ten pound franchise was the voting requirement. This eliminated the poorer and more rebellious people.

In the 1830s the landlords and their tenants were constantly at each other's throats. The unfortunate tenants found it difficult to come up with the exhorbitant rents, which led to them being evicted from their holdings. Feelings hardened, with murders and hangings following in the wake of dispossessions.

The biggest landlord/tenant problem stemmed from the absentee landlord. Travellers in Ireland at that time were struck by the number of empty, useless mansions. Millions of pounds in Irish rent money was being spent in England and on the Continent. Agents were appointed to look after the landlord's interests in the country. Their only brief was to come up with the required rent on time. The agent's commission came from anything extra they could bleed from the hapless tenants. Farms were continually being divided in ever decreasing segments in order to produce more rent. This in turn led to the tenants being unable to produce enough crops, even for their immediate family needs.

If one wished to outline some of the worst injustices and atrocities committed against the Irish by the English one could not find a better chronicler than Daniel O'Connell, MP. His *Memoir on Ireland Native and Saxon* makes telling reading and shows that the great statesman was under no illusion as to how the English behaved towards the Irish. The following are some typical extracts which reflect the happenings of the times:

The English dominion in Ireland commenced in the year 1172. It was for some centuries extended over only an inconsiderable portion of the island. From various causes the English district or Pale sometimes augmented in size, sometimes diminished. It did not become generally diffused over Ireland until the last years of Queen Elizabeth, nor universally so, until shortly after the accession of James the First. The success of the forces of Queen Elizabeth was achieved by means of the most horrible treachery, murder, wholesale massacre, and deliberately created famine. Take the last instance; the growing crops were year after year destroyed, until the fairest part of Ireland, and in particular the province of Munster, was literally depopulated. I give here one quotation. It is from the English Protestant historian Morrison: 'No spectacle was more frequent in the ditches of the towns, and especially in wasted countries, than to see multitudes of these poor people, the Irish, dead, with their mouths all coloured by eating nettles, docks, and all things they could rend above the ground.'

O'Connell went on as follows:
Never was a people on the face of the globe so cruelly treated as the Irish.

The Irish people were not received into allegiance or to the benefit of being recognised as subjects until the year 1612, only 228 years ago, when the Statute II James I. cap. 5, was enacted. The Statute abolished all distinctions of race between English and Irish, 'with the intent that,' as the Statute expresses it, 'they may grow into one nation, whereby there may be an utter obligation and extinguishment of all former differences and discord betwixt them.'

During the four hundred and forty years, that intervened between the commencement of the English dominion in 1172 and its completion in 1612, the Irish people were known only as 'Irish enemies'. They were denominated 'Irish Enemies' in all the Royal Proclamations, Royal Charters, and Acts of Parliament, during the period. It was their legal and technical description.

During that period the English were prohibited from intermarrying with the Irish, from having their children nursed by the wives of Irish Captains, Chiefs, or Lords; and what is still more strange, the English were also prohibited from sending goods, wares, or merchandises for sale, or selling them upon credit or for ready money to the Irish.

During that time any person of English descent might murder a mere Irish man or woman with perfect impunity. Such murder was no more a crime in the eye of the law, than the killing of a rabid or ferocious animal.

O'Connell goes on to extract and quote from official English sources how they set about depopulating the country. He notes 'that there were more than 100,000 persons of every age and sex banished'; of whom several thousand were, as he says, sent to the West India islands. We also learn from the original letter in the possession of Dr Lingard, that the vessels were crowded with the poorer classes of Catholics and sent to Barbados and other West India islands. 'I believe,' says the writer, 'that already sixty thousand are gone; for the husbands being first sent to Spain and Belgium, already their wives and children are destined for Americas.' It would be indeed idle to exclaim at any cruelty committed at that time. Those unhappy exiles perished in hundreds and thousands. Of the myriads thus transported, not a single one survived at the end of twenty years.

'Was there any species of crime which was not perpetrated against the Irish by the barbarians of the English Governments?' asks the great Liberator.

Many of these, of course, refer to the aftermath of the Treaty of Limerick when many Clare people were transported to the Barbados and the West Indies.

It is no wonder that the clergy were in constant hiding when we hear of such acts of law put into force by the English as the following:

> In the same year (1652) the Parliament commissioners at Dublin published a proclamation, signed Charles Fleetwood, Edmund Ludlow, and John Jones; wherein the acts of the 27th of Elizabeth was made of force in Ireland, and ordered to be most strictly put into execution. By this act, every Romish priest, so found, was deemed guilty of rebellion, and sentenced to be hanged until he was half dead; then to have his head taken off, and his body cut in quarters; his bowels to be drawn out and burned; and his head fixed upon a pole in some public place. (Curry's *Review,* page 392).

In the last chapter of his book O'Connell goes on to catalogue some of the chiefs and nobles slaughtered by the Protestants. Beginning with some illustrious chiefs from other parts of the country, we note that amongst them are Lord Hugh McMahon; Cornelius Maguire, Lord Viscount Iniskillen; the illustrious Felix O'Neill; Henry O'Neill, son of Eugene O'Neill; Thaddaeus O'Connor of Sligo, a descendant of the royal race, hung in Boyle, AD 1652.

In relation to some of the Clare chiefs who were cruelly betrayed, the following extract is worth recording:

> The illustrious Donat O'Brien, descended of the Royal race of the O'Briens, a most generous man, and of surpassing hospitality; after the Protestants had plighted to him their faith, and given him safe conduct in order that he might become their tributary; an attack being made one day by the Protestants against the Catholics, he (O'Brien) relying on his having been received into their friendship, approached; when a certain Protestant knight shot him through the body. Unsatisfied with this cruelty, when the old man (then about 64 years) had entered a hut, half dead, that he might in penitence commend himself to God, a soldier followed, set fire to the hut, and burned this noble old man — in Thomond AD 1651.
>
> James O'Brien, of illustrious lineage, maternal nephew of the aforesaid Donatus O'Brien, a youth of high hopes and prospects, was murdered at Nenagh by the Ormonds. They cut his head off and sent to his uterine brother, Moriarty O'Brien, then their prisoner.
>
> Bernard O'Brien, of the same noble family, a youth of equally fair prospects, was hanged in 1651.
>
> Daniel O'Brien, first cousin of the said Bernard, was hanged, and his head cut off at Nenagh, 1651.

There is one unusual activity which reached its zenith in the 1820s and 1830s — the lawless practice of faction fighting. It was little more than groups of families banding together to engage each other in battle with sticks and stones. The venues for these contests were the villages and towns to which the country folk would flock on fair days. Groups of hundreds confronted each other in the main street on the appointed day. With sticks and stones flying in all directions, it was a lucky man indeed who came away without injury.

The police and townspeople stayed well clear of these encounters. All shops and houses were boarded up to minimise damage to property. Faction fighting would appear to have been closely related to the old clan wars. Faction fighting started in Tipperary and it was also common in Limerick and Kerry, and to a lesser extent in Clare. A few interesting episodes which occurred in Clare are worth relating.

A fierce fight took place at the fair of Kildysart on 23 May 1825. When the buying and selling was completed, and some refreshments drunk, both factions faced each other. The Kildysart faction was led by Pat Moylan, Mick McInerney and Martin Keane, while the Ballinacally faction relied heavily on O'Donnell, Connor, Quinn and Walsh. Moylan struck James O'Donnell the first blow which was enough to unleash the warring factions on each other. A group of twenty led by Martin Keane from Kildysart, found the going tough so that at one stage Keane himself had to face the formidable trio of Quinn, Walsh and Connor. Expert though Keane was, he was hard put to ward off three good men. When the stick was knocked from his grasp by an elbow stroke from Walsh, he quickly stooped to pick it up. At the very same instant Quinn and Connor were delivering blows which they were not able to check, and he was struck a heavy blow on the side of the head. Keane fell unconscious with a fractured skull and was trampled on by the crowd. Towards the end of the evening, O'Driscoll of the Ballinacallys stunned McInerney who was a very skilful fighter on the other side. Finally, with an uppercut of his large blackthorn stick he practically lifted Moylan off his feet and stretched him out in the dust. This ended the contest and both factions were completely exhausted. They all agreed that it was a great fight and regretted that Martin Keane had been badly hurt. In fact Keane later died of his injuries.

Over in Killaloe the Corbans and Hourigans had tussled in some notable faction fights. After the big fair of Killaloe on 21 April 1829, three men lay dead in Ballina, just across the Shannon from Killaloe. The military made an unsuccessful attempt to stop the fighting there. When they fired into the crowd, John Minogue and Thady Moloney of the Corbans faction, and Stephan Hinchey of the Hourigans, all small farmers, were shot dead. Sergeant William Browne was convicted of the wilful murder of Hinchey, but was later acquitted at the Clonmel assizes. Four of the faction leaders were also arraigned before a judge and jury in Clonmel and were each sentenced to two years imprisonment for their parts in the riot.

The practice of faction fighting continued on a sliding scale until the middle of the nineteenth century when it died out almost completely. Memories of the factions have lingered in some places. Some recent-day family feuds have been reignited with little more than the shouting of an old faction battle cry.

This decade also saw the building of national schools in the county. Some money could be earned by the poor in the construction of these schools. Fast on the heels of the schools came the erection of the workhouses. There was one situated in each of the following locations:— Ennis, Kilrush, Scariff and Ennistymon.

Daniel O'Connell felt that if the Union were replaced and Ireland left to run her own affairs she would be well able to feed her people. To gain further support for his ideas he held huge outdoor meetings around the country. The first such meeting was held at Ballycoree just near Ennis, in 1843. Reports of the day say that roads to Ennis were jammed with enthusiastic Catholics converging on the hill near Ennis. Once again Clare was the hub of patriotic feelings with the entire country looking to it as the hotbed of Irish sentiment. One hundred bandsmen led the procession, and brilliant sunshine added to the enjoyment of a perfect rally. Clare's contribution to the Repeal Rent fund amounted to £1,200. A banquet was held afterwards in the Old Chapel in Ennis.

More monster meetings followed in other parts of Ireland, but the repeal year of 1843 went out without the movement realising its objective. The Irish and English Union was not repealed. As pointed out earlier, three adverse conditions could spell disaster for Ireland and by 1845 the three misfortunes had blended together to decimate the Irish people. The Union had not been repealed, therefore Ireland could not control her own affairs. Secondly, the population had increased phenomenally from a little over half a million in 1651 to approximately eight to nine million people by 1845. Thirdly, the principal food of the Irish peasant, the potato, rotted in the pits towards the end of 1845. A wail of despondency went up from the Irish people for they knew what was in store for them.

Failure of the potato crop was always a puzzle, even in England and on the Continent. Writing from Devon, Jas. Barnes told of total failure there. After careful examination of his own crop, he came to the conclusion that the original cause of the disease was still unknown. He was, however, fairly convinced that the trouble started in the tubers and spread from there. He could not have been more wrong of course, as the following twentieth century discovery explains.

The potato crop failed due to an attack by Phytophtora Infestans, or more commonly called blight. Three quarters of a century later it was discovered that it was a whitish growth on potato leaves which developed when weather conditions became wet and humid. Nothing less than your renowned 'soft day' aided and abetted the culprit germ. The disease was also capable of being transferred indirectly to the tubers by being washed down to and through the ground, from the leaves. The 1845 crop was infected after digging, while the harvest of 1846 was rotten in the ground.

The *Clare Journal* of 19 January 1846, urged the gentlemen of Clare to grow their potato crops early. Being late in tillage was injurious to the crop, the *Journal* stated. It was further asserted that the gentlemen of Clare should make some exertion themselves rather than suggesting to the Government ways in which the land might be improved. As common and as vital as the potato was, surprisingly very little was known of its peculiarities.

With no rent being paid, widespread evictions followed. Roofs were torn from the tiny cabins in one sweep with grappling hooks. Sometimes an entire village would be de-roofed, throwing all the undernourished occupants to the merciless weather. The despoiled people huddled in dreadfully wet ditches with the remains of their original roofing propped overhead. This type of habitation was commonly called a 'scalp'. Much of the population lived in scalps for too many years in famine times. It would not be unrealistic to

Finely constructed abutment walls, the result of famine relief works, on the river Fergus, just north of Ballyalla Lake, near Ennis.

assume that the present day itinerant is a hangover from scalp conditions.

When the people looked over their blackened fields in '46 a mood of despair overcame them. Relief works were put into operation by the authorities to provide income for the needy. With wages ranging from six to ten pence per day, families were hardly able to feed themselves, not even once every second day.

At the Clare Abbey relief works the overseer, a Mr Hennessy, was shot and wounded by an unknown and distraught man. The works were suspended in an attempt to bring the man responsible to the authorities. Much suffering followed in the villages of Clare as the people were without relief. Time passed but nobody would name the assailant. Finally, a Captain Wynne intervened by sending pleading letters to the Board of Works and to Lord Trevelyan. A quote from the documents would give an accurate description of general conditions in Clare at the end of December 1846:

> Although a man not easily moved, I confess myself unmanned by the intensity and extent of the suffering I witnessed more especially among the women and little children, crowds of whom were to be seen scattered over the turnip fields like a flock of banished crows, devouring the raw turnips, mothers half naked, shivering in the snow and sleet, muttering exclamations of despair while their children were screaming with hunger.

The works at Clare Abbey were reopened on 28 December 1846.

The workhouses became rapidly overcrowded. A new one had to be constructed in Tulla. Conditions in those fearful institutions were most unhygienic. More often than not cholera overtook those battling against starvation. The Kilrush Union was particularly bad where hundreds of paupers were dying each month. It was little wonder that people died there for when the costs of running the workhouse are examined, we find that it took 11½d. to feed a pauper each week. Children were reared and educated in the unsuitable surroundings of the workhouses. A school mistress in the Ennis Union received a yearly salary of £15, with ration, coal and candles.

Soups and stirabout were dispensed at population centres around the country. Although the people were dying on their feet they could not abide the shame of queueing for soup with bowl or pot in hand. The people of Ennistymon said they had no bowls, such was their pride. At Miltown Malbay a crowd rushed the kitchen and demolished the boiler.

Many benevolent better off people did their best to get food to the hungry. The Society of Friends did trojan work in their efforts to relieve the starving. Donations came from America and England to buy food for the people. But these offers, welcome though they were, were but a pebble to a quarry. For every ship England sent up the Shannon to supply the district with grain, six were leaving the country bound for England. Ireland was exporting enough food to feed twice the population! Such was English policy.

The Ennis relief fund of 31 March 1846, which was published in the *Clare Journal* showed that there were numerous Clare contributors. Topping the list was a Mr Joseph Gore with a donation of £50. Mr Vandeleur made a similar contribution to the Kilrush Union.

The famine of '46 and '47, the Great Hunger, left much hatred behind. It cleaved like a sword through the Irish and English connection like nothing before or since. Its effect stretches right into present times. Irish people are still prepared to admonish England with a sense of grief which belongs to those who feel they have personally endured the tragedy. It reached out to relations between England and Ireland when the Second World War broke out. Ireland remained neutral, refusing to ally herself with England because it was no longer believed that England was synonymous with freedom.

Meanwhile, outside Clare, O'Connell was prosecuted for holding one of his popular meetings in Clontarf, Dublin. His arrest quickly led to his falling from political prominence. The Young Irelanders then took up the political cudgel. They were more disposed to using violence should the need arise. The British were very well aware that O'Connell would not resort to violence of any kind, and they used this fact to the detriment of his political aspirations. The great parliamentarian died on 15 May 1847 at Genoa, while travelling to Rome. A famous Clareman, William Smith O'Brien, gained leadership of the revolutionary movement shortly after O'Connell's death.

By the time the famine was over in 1851, an estimated two and a half million persons were lost in it throughout Ireland. In Clare the figure could have been as high as 70,000 — almost the equivalent of the present population.

The revolutionary Fenian Movement started in the 1860s, and it had organisations both in the United States and in Ireland. Many of Clare's sons returned from the American civil war to give clandestine military instructions to those at home. Weapons of war were supposed to be secretly imported into the

A boat being unloaded at Clarecastle Harbour at the end of the last century. Note the excellent condition of the castle and barracks in the background. (Lawrence Collection 6466 National Library).

country and put in hiding for the 'Rising'. The 5 March 1867 was the night fixed for general rebellion. Many thousands of Claremen were out in their appointed positions, but no weapons or large scale plan materialised. There was a small skirmish at Kilbaha coastguard station. Some volunteers were betrayed in a grove near Ennis when one of their number struck a match to signal the authorities.

Charles Stewart Parnell, leader of the Irish MPs to Westminster, made his famous 'boycott' speech at Ennis, in 1882, for which he was subsequently imprisoned. In 1884 he returned to Miltown Malbay at the request of Rev P. White. (He was the priest who wrote a very comprehensive history of Clare). Charles S. Parnell addressed a huge gathering on the lawn of the parochial hall, on the much agitated Land Question. A huge crowd listened to Parnell while they basked in glorious sunshine, with banners flying and the music of many bands adding to the festivities. The main objective of the Land League was to acquire Fixity of Tenure for the small farmers. Work on the railway line was officially commenced by him when he ceremoniously turned the first sod there. Both he and the nineteenth century passed without self-government coming to the country.

In this century many buildings, which are still standing, were constructed. The Christian Brothers built their schools about the middle of the century in Ennis and Ennistymon. The diocesan college of St Flannan on the southern side of Ennis was also erected. Girls were catered for in schools of the Sisters of Mercy. When the original courthouse fell into bad repair an imposing new building was constructed in Lifford, Ennis, in 1852. The site of the old building accommodated the 74 foot high column holding the statue of Daniel O'Connell. The 'Monument' as it is now known, was worked from limestone by Ennis sculptor, Cahill. It was unveiled on the 3 October 1865 by Dr Power, Bishop of Killaloe.

Although there had been a slight increase in prosperity after the Crimean War, famine struck the county in the wet summers of 1863 and 1864. This outbreak was not nearly as bad as 1846 and 1847, but there were many cases of suffering on a lesser scale.

Conditions improved somewhat towards the end of the century with increased prices for cattle and butter. However, the commercial structure of the country was still very weak. Ireland would have to rule herself if she were to make any progress.

In the last quarter of the nineteenth century the English Tory Government banned the Land League. This resulted in secret meetings to plan illegal activities. There was much coercive action against the Clare farming class during this time. In spite of the ban, some meetings were held in Ennis, Kilrush and Miltown Malbay.

Turnpike Road Ennis around 1900. The dwellings shown were demolished in the mid-twentieth century to make way for MacNamara and Dalcassian Parks. (Lawrence collection 6265, National Library).

Rents were withheld as a protest against coercion. Evictions followed in some places. Amongst the more infamous occurrences, were those of Bodyke and Miltown Malbay. Some tenants in Bodyke barricaded themselves in their cabins, and steadfastly refused to leave their land. The police arrived and much excitement followed. Shots were discharged before an amicable solution was reached. In Miltown-Malbay a protracted struggle took place. It was made all the more troublesome by an agent re-letting land from which a tenant had been evicted. However, after some considerable time the fracas died out.

Undoubtedly, the nineteenth century must have been the blackest in the history of Clare. Starvation and a landless people were the plight of the once proud and fighting Dalcassians. They were still without a national government, but the desire to regain local rule was ever present.

The first step towards native administration was won from Westminister in 1898. The local Government Act of that year gave the country her County and Urban Councils. This was the beginning of the Clare County Council and the Urban Councils as we know them today.

A drift from the land had commenced early in this century. Clare people were flocking to explore and settle in America and Australia; and of course, to work in Britain. Nevertheless, the population was substantial enough in the latter part of the 1800s, and stood at about 130,000 inhabitants. The question was, therefore, could a dwindling, down trodden people, arise to re-establish their own government? For once the will was not in Clare, but it was elsewhere.

Chapter 10

The Fight for Freedom (1900 — 1924)

The present century began in much the same fashion as the previous one left off. People continued to exist on small patches of land and attempted to support large families. Poverty was still widespread, as can be seen from the following *Clare Journal* report of Thursday, 9 January 1908:

> At the weekly meeting of the Board of Guardians of the Ennis Union, the Chairman Mr P.E. Keanneally presided. A report on the state of the house went as follows:- Admitted 35; Born 0; Discharged 37; Died 4; Remaining in the House 44, at an average cost of 4s.-2½d.; Number in infirmary 96 at a general cost of 5s.-4½d.; In fever hospital 2 at an average cost of 10s.-3d. Tramps admitted 15 men, 4 women and 9 children.

Many of Clare's towns and villages were made up of merchants and publicans. There was very little urban development, because employment, other than agricultural labouring, was very scarce. Paradoxically, some relief was experienced in the county when the First World War broke out in 1914. Because there was little employment at home many of Clare's sons joined the British Army. Wages, and for the unfortunate, pensions, flowed into the country from the soldiers fighting abroad.

Another step towards normal civil rights was received when the 1903 Land Act was put into operation. This piece of legislation gave a new measure of freedom to the farmers. It enabled the tenant farmers to buy back their holdings from the landlords by a system of annuities. The British Government made special grants to compensate the landowners against any losses. This was an important breakthrough because it ensured fixity of tenure in the holdings, fairer rents were fixed and the right of free sale was guaranteed.

The west coast of Clare continued to be unhospitable to seafarers. Another shipwreck occurred off Spanish Point on 14 January 1916. A three masted schooner, *Kelp,* was smashed on the rocks. Fortunately the crew were rescued and received very good treatment from the local people. This was in stark contrast to the reception offered to the unfortunate victims of the Spanish Armada some centuries earlier.

In Easter week of 1916 the blow struck for Irish freedom reverberated around the country. The revolution was Dublin based and was not a military success. It did, however, lead to independence for twenty-six counties. This then was the road back from a very dark wilderness. Because of the dilution of provincial power — the dissipation of the clans for the central authority of England — rebellions became ideologically based. If the *Clare Champion* editorial of 6 May 1916, is anything to go by, most people of the time did not comprehend the significance of that historic event in Ireland's capital city. 'The Dublin revolution has come and gone — gone to join the shades of many another attempt on the part of desperate Irishmen to establish an Irish Republic.' The Bishop of Killaloe preaching at Quin referred to the Dublin troubles by bewailing and lamenting the mad adventure, but he did give them credit for dying bravely even if foolishly. However, the cruel execution of the leaders had a significant effect on public opinion and later swayed many to sympathise with the freedom fighters.

World opinion caused the British Government to release all prisoners by early 1917, which was the signal for a new wave of political activity. Later on the night of 23 June 1917, marks a historic arrival at Ennis railway station. The train from Dublin brought the hero of Boland's Mills (Easter Week revolution), Eamon de Valera. He came to Clare at the bequest of the Sinn Féin organisation to contest a by-election caused by the death of Major William Redmond. Major Redmond had been parliamentary MP for East Clare since 1892.

The train was greeted with fog signals and flags in a crowded Ennis station. On the roadway outside one thousand volunteers were assembled to show their undying allegiance to the cause of self-government. A historic association had begun between man and county. Eamon de Valera had commenced his campaign for the Sinn Féin cause in Clare. It was a campaign that would have long and far reaching effects.

Commandant de Valera's maiden speech in the political arena was made in Clare on that very same night. He addressed a crowd of enthusiastic supporters at Sinn Féin headquarters, the Old Ground Hotel, before retiring. The crowd was ecstatic and greeted his every sentence with 'Up Dev' and 'We'll put him in.'

A campaign of political rallies began and continued with great intensity right up to polling day on 10 July 1917. A disturbing incident occurred on the first day of the campaign when Sinn Féin supporters were motoring between Broadford and Tuamgraney. On stopping to clear an obstruction on the road they came under attack from rifle fire. Fifteen rounds in all were fired on them, one piercing the vehicle's petrol tank. None of the party was injured and they eventually arrived in Tuamgraney in time for their political rally. Appeals from the Very Rev P.J. Hogan Adm., Ennis, and from Mr G. McElroy RM to remain calm and to conduct the campaign with dignity seemingly was taken to heart, for no serious incident occurred thereafter.

Some prominent speakers who supported De Valera and the Sinn Féin cause in the Clare campaign included; Professor Eoin McNeill, Larry Ginnell MP, Peadar Clancy, Arthur Griffiths, Séan Milroy, Count Plunkett, T.V. Honan, and many local political and clerical dignitaries.

In opposition to Sinn Féin was Mr Patrick Lynch KC, representing the Irish

Party. He came from a very respected and well connected Clare family, and in most circumstances he would have been an excellent representative. But after centuries of oppression the 1916 rising had cast off the yoke of foreign domination and this put the people in the mood for change.

As the campaign started, parades and street rallies, especially in Ennis, were commonplace. The Sinn Féin supporters waved the Tricolour while supporters of the Irish Party and Mr Lynch usually had green flags, sometimes the French colours and the Union Jack. On Monday 25 June, a clash between police and the rallyists occurred at O'Connell Square, Ennis. The police baton-charged the crowd which resulted in minor injuries to some of them.

On 10 July voting took place at Ennis courthouse. Early voters included Dr Michael Fogarty, Bishop of Killaloe, and Very Rev Canon O'Dea, President of St Flannan's College, Ennis. During an incident outside the Ennis Town Hall polling booth some men were injured in a scuffle. They were given first aid by Countess Markievicz and Dr MacClancy of Ennis. Incidents continued right into the night and it became unsafe to walk the streets of the Clare capital.

When the count was made known on the following day by Sheriff Major F.G. Cullinan it was: De Valera, 5,010 votes: Lynch, 2,035 votes. A clear-cut victory for De Valera and Sinn Féin which reverberated throughout the country. Clare had once again struck against the old enemy by consolidating the freedom fighters through the ballot box. This victory ensured great support for Sinn Féin and it convinced the neutrals that self determination was not only possible but the only way forward.

Success at the polls was the signal for further drilling and training of volunteers. In all areas men were being taught the rudiments of soldiering. This was done in open defiance of the authorities such as the Royal Irish Constabulary. Many local military leaders were arrested but all to no avail as the enthusiastic volunteers continued their recruiting and training.

In September De Valera returned to Clare to rally the people after the death of Thomas Ashe in Dublin. In a famous speech he said:

> Since I was last in Clare, I have visited many parts of Ireland and everywhere I went I heard the words 'Good old Clare' and 'Brave old Clare'. Everywhere I went I found the enthusiasm and spirit almost as strong as in Clare. The same determination is alive all over the country today as in the brave boys of Ennis and Clare who are bravely and unflinchingly defying the Sasanach in his prisons and it shows that there is no breaking the spirit that is alive in the hearts of Irishmen.
>
> As I came along the streets I saw the illuminations and the great enthusiasm displayed by the gathering, but I also observed that the flags were draped in black. I thought of the many times Brian of old went out with his brave Dalcassians to battle and came back victorious but at the same time mourning the loss of brave comrades who fell in the fight. If victory in Ireland has to be purchased at the cost of draping our flags, then let it be so, but victory we shall have and that determination which is in our hearts no enemy can crush.

The next day a mass meeting with 20,000 to 25,000 people assembled in or about the Square in Ennis where the support for the commandant was ecstatic to say the least. He was being recognised as the Commander-in-Chief of the Sinn Féin army. Thereafter he was frequently and affectionately referred to as 'The Chief'.

The year 1918 saw the development of a new activity in Clare as in other parts of Ireland. The Sinn Féin volunteers were advocating total severance from British Authority — the removal of all vestiges of British rule, such as police, army, local government officials, etc. They lacked the arms to form any kind of effective fighting force, so the practice of stealing weapons and ammunition began on a wide scale. Irishmen home on leave from the British Army were a favourite target for the volunteers.

Again, it seems that it was the men of Clare who led the way in fresh guerrilla activity when an RIC hut was attacked at Inch on 8 January. This was the first such attack in the county. Local Sinn Féin volunteers attacked the hut to procure whatever arms and ammunition might be inside. After a number of shots were fired the volunteers withdrew without success, fearing that reinforcements may have been sent from Ennis.

Another development which occurred in 1918 was the practice of cattle drives. Volunteers drove off cattle from the lands of Crown sympathisers, proving a great disruption to their farming and domestic lives. On one such drive at Castlefergus, John Ryan of Newmarket-on-Fergus was shot in the back and later died of his wounds in the Ennis infirmary. A number of other men were wounded in the same incident.

Many men were arrested during this period of unrest, and included amongst others: H.J. Hunt (Commandant Fifth Battalion, Clare Brigade); Michael Murray (Commandant First Battalion); Art O'Donnell (Commandant Seventh Battalion); Frank Gallagher (Vice-Commandant First Battalion); John Moynihan (Captain, A Company, Fifth Battalion); John Murnane (Captain, B Company, First Battalion); J.J. Liddy (Captain, G Company, Seventh Battalion); Michael O'Brien (Lieutenant, C Company Fifth Battalion); Peter O'Loughlin (Lieutenant, B Company, Sixth Battalion); Tom Browne (A Company, Fourth Battalion); James Madigan (A Company, Fourth Battalion); William McNamara (A Company, Fourth Battalion); Thomas Callaghan (E Company, Fourth Battalion); Thomas Marrinan (F Company, Fifth Battalion); Frank Shinnors (A Company, Fourth Battalion); as well as Paddy, Michael and Austin Brennan, and Jimmy Griffey. All of the above were prisoners in Mountjoy Jail in Dublin, at one time or another.

Towards the end of 1918 the Westminster Parliament was dissolved and the 14 December was fixed as polling day for the new election. It was immediately obvious that there was only one likely candidate for the East Clare constituency and that was Eamon de Valera.

At an election meeting in O'Connell Square, Ennis, the Rev William O'Kennedy of St Flannan's College gave a long address in which he wholeheartedly supported De Valera as a candidate. However, he did stress the Clare yearning for complete and undiluted freedom and that no representative, not even Eamon de Valera, would be allowed 'sully the flag like the Redmonds and the Dillions'. If that happened he continued: 'We Dalcassians will tear the idol out of our hearts and smash it to the ground, because it is contrary to the principles for which our forefathers fought and for which we will fight on. But, men of Clare, De Valera is not a man who will massage the body of old John Bull.' He went on to read a letter of support from the Most Rev Dr Fogarty who strongly condemned England for 'its plutocratic record of oppression, corruption and chicanery.'

As De Valera and Brian O'Higgins were the only nominees for their respective constituencies in Clare, both were returned without contest. Both men were prisoners in English jails at the time. The absence of the candidates from the campaign field greatly reduced interest and atmosphere in the proceedings.

The latter part of 1919 saw the people of Clare and Ireland clamouring for the release of Irish prisoners of war who were detained in British jails. There was much excitement when it was learned that Clare's own hero, Eamon de Valera, had escaped from Lincoln prison and had been spirited to America. There was more rejoicing in the west Clare area when Brian O'Higgins came home from Birmingham jail.

Guerrilla action continued throughout the county. The barracks at Newmarket-on-Fergus was raided in August and RIC men were tied to their beds. A small quantity of revolvers, rifles and ammunition was seized. The Newmarket action was the first success of its kind in the county, and it was led by Michael Brennan, O/C East Clare Flying Column. Broadford barracks was also put under siege. Raids continued at Islandbawn, Kilkee, Ennistymon, and a police patrol was ambushed in the Kilmihil area. A youth died in the Ennistymon raid and two RIC men were shot in the Islandbawn Protection Hut incident. More barracks to come under attack included Kilfenora, Doonbeg and Lissycasey RIC Hut. A police patrol was fired upon in the Ballyvaughan district.

The British Authorities were becoming concerned at the increased level of guerrilla activity in the county and sent in reinforcements and additional equipment. Armoured cars and Crossely tenders were becoming commonplace on the roads of Clare. By April 1920 most RIC huts throughout the county had been put to the torch. In Miltown Malbay the police fired into a crowd, killing three people including a well-known Clare footballer, Patrick Hennessy. The Protestant church at Clarecastle was also burned by the Sinn Féin volunteers. As hostilities continued unabated the British sent two destroyers up the Shannon and landed fifty men of the Royal Marine Light Infantry at Kilrush. Nevertheless the volunteers continued without letup.

March 1920 saw the introduction of that infamous auxilliary force — the Black and Tans. The 'Tans' became known for their cruelty and the many atrocities they committed throughout the land.

A Constable Lockheed was killed during the taking of the RIC barracks at Ruan in October 1920. In November four volunteers were shot dead 'while trying to escape' on the bridge at Killaloe. They were John Egan, age 26; Michael McMahon, age 26; Martin Kildea, age 27; and Alfred Rogers, age 22. By December the authorities were becoming desperate and they raided Westbourne house, the bishop's residence. Fortunately, his Lordship was away at the time.

Seemingly, the volunteers had become bolder in their exploits, because two members of the Black and Tans went missing during the campaign. The following note was taken from the gates of the Old Ground Hotel, Ennis, just before the hotel was sacked and its furniture burned in the grounds:

LAST WARNING

If the two constables who were kidnapped at Ruan on the morning of the 15 inst. are not returned by midnight the 21st. to Ennis those who have received such former notices can prepare to meet their God.

Black and Tan.

The original note may still be seen in the museum section of Ennis Library.

One unusual incident which occurred at that time was the cruel if amateurish execution of a magistrate by the volunteers in Miltown Malbay. The man was buried alive up to his neck in the beach there. He was, however, positioned above the high water mark and the volunteers found him alive when they returned the following day. He was promptly reburied, this time facing the tide, which drowned him.

Martial law was proclaimed in January 1921, but still the war action continued without letup. The tension of the times may be glimpsed by relating an incident which occurred during curfew. A young girl in Ennis who was returning with a can of milk after curfew had the can shot from her hands by British soldiers. Without doubt, no person was trusted in those times when it was difficult to ascertain when the next attack might occur. Shooting at children and into crowds of civilians was not a practice which enhanced the reputation of the British forces in Ireland. As De Valera had said in an earlier speech to his constituents, 'If ever a people deserved freedom and the right to live out their lives unfettered, surely it was the Irish.'

On the political front another election was scheduled for 13 May. This was to send four TDs to a free parliament (The Dáil) in Dublin. The nominees who were elected unopposed and without fuss, were: Professor de Valera; John Liddy, farmer, Danganelly, Cooraclare; Patrick Brennan, clerk, Meelick; and Brian O'Higgins, author, Carrigaholt. Peace efforts were also being advanced at this time and finally a nation-wide truce was agreed and came into effect at 12 noon on 11 July, 1921.

Eamon de Valera and the Sinn Féin organisation kept the volunteers on standby in the county while the representatives of the country were locked in discussions with the British about the outcome of the war. A treaty was signed on 6 December to accept a partitioned country. All internees were then released. However, much dissension followed because the delegates had failed to win a thirty-two county republic from England. When votes on this issue were taken at council meetings throughout the county (as elsewhere) there were divisions, but there was enough support to ratify the treaty. This was done on 7 January 1922, by Dáil Éireann. President de Valera resigned.

A division occurred in the ranks of Sinn Féin between those who were for ratification and those against. Supporting the treaty were Michael Collins, Arthur Griffith, Richard Mulcahy, and Michael Brennan from Clare. Against the treaty were Eamon de Valera, Cathal Brugha, Liam Mellows, Commandant Frank Barrett, Mid-Clare Brigade, and Brian O'Higgins. Heated debates continued with De Valera strongly urging the Dalcassians to rally round the flag with their support.

An uneasy peace under the truce lasted into April 1922 when an ex-RIC Sergeant, John Gunn was shot dead in Lower Market Street, Ennis. Minor incidents continued for some months until the symptoms of civil war manifested themselves in an incident in Carron where a mother of nine was shot and died, seemingly without explanation. Fighting broke out in the Four Courts in Dublin and institutionalised groups like the Ennis banks became nervous and closed their doors for a short time to all customers. Ennis RIC barracks was partially looted on 6 July by a large crowd of women and children.

The Free State Army began night patrols and movement of the population was severely restricted. Lorries containing Free State troops were attacked near Ennis while the railway line at Corofin was torn up. All roads and bridges, including railway bridges leading to Corofin, were damaged and the village was partially isolated for a time. Free State Army posts (pro-treaty), taken over from the British, came under constant attack from anti-treaty troops. Skirmishes and personal attacks continued at a regular rate with killings, injuries and property damage being the end results.

In September 1922 the first Civic Guards under the command of Superintendant O'Dwyer arrived in the Clare capital. By the end of October the force stood at 63 men, ten sergeants and three inspectors. They were by then in authority in Ennis, Ennistymon, Kilrush, Lisdoonvarna, Sixmilebridge, Tulla, Kildysart, Kilkee and Killaloe.

The old West Clare Railway was attacked between Kilmurry and Craggaknock and the passengers were made to disembark. Many more attacks by Republican troops were carried out on the railway lines throughout the county, which had the effect of disrupting mail and restricting travel for the civilian population. Although it received many setbacks the old West Clare Railway managed to quickly bounce back anew and provide that timeless meandering service for which it was justly famous.

Attacks on Free State troops in the Ennis area were now frequent, resulting in injuries and deaths. Some soldiers on the anti-treaty side executed by the authorities included William O'Shaughnessy, Christie Quinn and Patrick O'Mahony. The old Home Barracks in the Kilrush Road was often used as a place of execution.

Frank Aiken, Chief of Staff of the Republican Army, ordered a suspension of all hostilities on 30 April. Towards the end of May matters had quietened down considerably and parties once again began to turn their attentions towards preparing for another general election. On this occasion Labour chose two candidates to contest the election, Patrick Hogan and P.J. McNamara. The farmers selected three candidates while Sinn Féin put forward Eamon de Valera, T.V. Honan, Frank Barrett, Brian O'Higgins and Michael Comyn KC. Supporters of the treaty under the banner of Cumann na Gael elected the following to contest the election for them:— Dr Eoin McNeill, P. Kelly PC from Cree, James O'Regan, Michael Hehir and Peadar O'Loughlin. The date for the general election was set for 27 August 1923.

Of course the main bone of contention for the election protagonists was partition — the Northern Ireland problem which was clearly anti united Ireland. At a Sinn Féin rally on 15 August, Eamon de Valera was arrested by the military and taken to the Home Barracks in the Kilrush Road, Ennis. Hundreds of people were injured when a stampede developed at the appearance of the military who had an armoured car on which was mounted a Lewis machine gun. A quiet election followed on 27 August and De Valera, then in Arbour Hill prison, headed the poll with 17,762 votes. After many counts under the proportional representation system the following were deemed elected: E. de Valera (S.F.), Eoin McNeill (C.G.), Brian O'Higgins (S.F.), C. Hogan (Farmers), P. Hogan (Labour).

For the next nine months or so many of the republicans were in Irish jails, including De Valera and O'Higgins. A massive public campaign was initiated to free all prisoners of war and by 16 July 1924, De Valera himself had been released. He returned at once to Clare amid bonfires and great celebrations on 15 August, the anniversary of his arrest. He continued to observe that anniversary date on his many visits to Ennis and Clare down through the years. He could be seen regularly on 15 August at the Clare Agricultural Show in the Showgrounds, Ennis. He always stood tall and defiant, as if remembering the old days of confrontation, even though his eyesight was failing during his visits in the 1960s and the 1970s. At that famous meeting of 1924 in the old town of Ennis, De Valera's words were received and repeated with great enthusiasm by the massive crowd. He was *the* man for the people of Clare.

The determined nature of Eamon de Valera was uniquely suited to that brilliant but simplistic feature of the Dalcassian character — their childlike belief in the right of freedom and their right to achieve that freedom. The Dalcassians had found and adopted a leader to carry out their ultimate wishes and anybody less direct than De Valera would not do. Not since Brian Boru had the Dalcassians had such a successful leader and he achieved exactly for them what his famous predecessor alone achieved — their much-loved independence.

It mattered little that De Valera's character would not allow him to take a softer role in the treaty debate. He could only be one way — direct, simple, achieve the goal at all costs. The Dalcassians could stand for no other complicated nonsense. It was good enough to obtain for them their freedom from a most belligerent and tenacious oppressor.

Chapter 11

Progress
(1925 — 1986)

After the hostilities had ceased it became the immediate task of the new government in the country to maintain and develop whatever infrastructure was already there. The country at the time was still in a somewhat primitive state. Although the motor car was beginning to make its appearance on some roads, the usual mode of transportation was the pony and trap or the bicycle. The economy of the time was almost totally based on agriculture, and even this sector found it difficult to make a decent living. After years of foreign domination, it seems that Ireland was reluctant to venture too far abroad with its development ideas. A programme of self-reliance was put into practice. After many years of protectionism and the lack of new technologies, the country began to fall behind in international trade. When the 1950s arrived, and an enlightened national government decided on industrial expansion, they found themselves with much ground to make up.

When the British occupation forces pulled out of the country there was no national electricity scheme in operation. There were a number of small private schemes in Dublin and in some other areas, but these were only adequate for small domestic users. Therefore, one of the very first requirements was the provision of a national electricity supply. Not surprisingly, the power of the Shannon was looked to as a likely source for electrical energy. Work commenced on the Ardnacrusha site in the hot summer of 1925, with a German firm supplying the technical expertise. Although there was a strike in the early days of the project, it did go on eventually to employ 5,000 men, some at the very low wage of 17s.-6d. per week. The power station was ready for use four years later and became operative on 24 October 1929. It is still in use today but has been superseded in importance by the bigger oil and coal burning stations in other parts of Ireland.

With the advent of the motor car on Irish roads came the emergence of new industries. Better roads had to be provided for the car, and additional employment was made available through the garages that serviced these vehicles.

In general though, living conditions were quite difficult in the 1930s and there seemed to be little hope for improvements in the future. One significant event was to change all that — the arrival of the aeroplane. This more than

Ennis before the motor car arrived. Picture of O'Connell Street.
(Lawrence Collection, National Library).

anything else, was responsible for launching Clare into the technological age. Because planes found it impossible to make the long Atlantic crossing to Europe without refuelling, it became necessary for them to take on more fuel in the westerly part of Ireland. This qualified Rineanna (from the Gaelic meaning 'The landing place of the birds') as the best location for an international airport. In 1936 construction work began on the 760 acre site quite close to the Shannon estuary. The runways were just completed in 1939 when the first aircraft touched down for a perfect three point landing. Between the period 1939 to 1945, services were confined to the Irish Air Corps who operated daily patrols. Passenger traffic through the airport in the 1940s increased until it became an interational attraction in 1947, when Shannon became the world's first Custom Free Airport. From this developed fine shops and a mail order company.

From the depths of pauperism in the recent past, Shannon Airport launched the county into world focus. Shannon, as the airport became known internationally, was *the* most important event to occur in the county in modern times. It went on to revitalise the entire area that was the old kingdom of Thomond. The man who did much to pioneer the development work was Brendan O'Regan from Sixmilebridge.

With the emergence of the long distance jet aircraft, the possibility arose that the airport would be overflown with a consequent loss of business. This caused some concern at first because of a feared loss of revenue and employment at Shannon. However, the Shannon Free Airport Development Authority were equal to the occasion when they established an industrial estate in the immediate vicinity of the airport zone. The incentive was given to foreign industrialists to establish their manufacturing firms in an area which would have many desirable economic conditions. Concessions and enticements were offered in the way of grants to build factories and buy machinery, and tax-free profits obtained for ten years. Grants were also provided for the training of workers.

The entire Shannon project was a very successful undertaking which attracted firms from the USA, England, Germany, Japan as well as many more countries. The factories provided thousands of jobs on the industrial estate and pretty soon the Development Company found it necessary to build a housing estate on Drumgeely Hill. This was to accommodate the many workers being drawn from all over Ireland and some from overseas to return with new hope. From this beginning the town of Shannon was born. In the centuries prior to that time, no new settlement had been established in the county. The foundation and growth of Shannon Town was truly the most encouraging hope for the future of Clare since the days of Brian Boru. Significantly, at the time of writing, Shannon has grown to be the second largest town in Clare with a population nearing 10,000 people. The industrial estate nearby contains over one hundred factories which are operating successfully.

'Flying Boats' at Foynes in the Shannon Estuary — the forerunner of Shannon Airport.

Not content with enticing industrialists, the Shannon Development team came up with the idea of bringing tourists to a medieval banquet at Bunratty Castle. The ruins of the once majestic fortress were restored to their former

Shannon — Clare's newest town. Picture shows early development in the nineteen sixties.

splendour in 1960 by Lord Gort. Commencing in 1963, the old halls of Bunratty rang to the sound of music and merriment when the banquets began. Ever since tourists have flocked from all parts of the world to wine and dine as did the Earls of Thomond in medieval days. Food is eaten in the authentic way — without the aid of utensils, and intoxicating mead is dispensed as in ancient times. Yes, there is much joviality at Bunratty these days — a far cry from the times when men were hanged from battlements, or drawn between horses!

Under the shadow of Bunratty's ancient walls, the village inn also prospers. 'Durty Nelly's' must be one of the oldest and busiest pubs in the country. An abundance of cars rather than horses, may be seen every day patiently awaiting their masters outside the hostelry. The new Irish 'peasant' can live it up in the way of the long forgotten nobility.

Although the ancient game of hurling was always with us, it was not organised into a proper field sport until the end of the last century. The Gaelic Athletic Association was founded by the Burren man, Michael Cusack. From then on both hurling and Gaelic football were regulated by rules, and played on a standard size field. Prior to that the games had been played by pursuing a ball from parish to parish. Clare won its only All Ireland Senior Hurling title in 1914. A senior football title has so far eluded the county.

Some traditional customs which have survived and even gained strength in the twentieth century are Irish dancing and traditional music. The middle decades of this century are renowned for the popularity of ballroom dancing

Shannon Industrial Estate.

throughout Ireland. Every town and village had its dance hall and the arrival of a big-time band was the highlight of the week. The more traditional dances and music were fostered by groups of far-seeing people like Comhaltas Ceoltóirí Éireann. Many of the old tunes and dances have been preserved and made famous by such purists as the late Willie Clancy of Miltown Malbay. Clare has become the stronghold of traditional music with areas like Miltown Malbay and Doolin being descended upon each summer by Irish music lovers in search of the 'real thing' — many coming from Scandinavia and continental Europe.

Perhaps one of the last great reminders of earlier times was the fair held each year in the fairgreen, Ennis. This once wide field (now a sportsfield and playground) was converged on and filled from end to end with cattle. From morning until nightfall individual needs were bargained for, culminating only in the traditional slapping of the palms. The residents of the town, not to mention the school children nearby, gained little respite from the bawling of cattle which could be heard for many miles around. This great event was dispensed with when Clare Marts Ltd were set up to provide regular cattle sales on a more orderly basis. Maybe the Cleansing and Sanitation department of the local Council was relieved to see the winding up of this annual event!

The railway which was laid through Clare in the last century is still here. The main line runs through Ennis, from Limerick, and on to Galway. Unfortunately, the county's famous narrow gauge artery has long since disappeared.

Ardnacrusha Power Station during construction in 1928.

The line of the old West Clare Railway ran from Ennis to Kilkee, via Corotin and Lahinch. Some of its excursions to Lahinch proved too trying for the turn-of-the-century steam engine — the passengers were often obliged to get out and push at the steeper gradients! The 'West Clare' has been immortalised in Percy French's famous song, 'Are you right there Michael?' A sad decision was taken when Córas Iompar Éireann had the link ripped up and sold to the emerging country, Nigeria, in 1960. The reasons given for this piece of destruction was 'economic viability'.

The new industrial employment in Shannon also meant prosperity for the old town of Ennis. Large urban developments in the way of housing schemes were built in Hermitage, Ard na Greine, and the Lifford area. In 1956 a floor in one of the older buildings, Carmody's Hotel in Abbey Street, collapsed while an auction was in progress. Eight people were killed in the accident and many others injured. Eamon de Valera sometimes stayed in the hotel when he had occasion to visit Clare. The site of the building has since been cleared to make a larger entrance to the car park opposite the present Queen's Hotel.

A picture of the commercial development of the county may be gleaned from the fact that around 1900, barges on the River Fergus were still plying goods between Ennis and Limerick. Those long flat-bottomed vessels could be manoeuvred right up the Fergus into the centre of Ennis. Unloading took place at the back of Parnell Street at Wood Quay. The river around Ennis was much more tidal than it is today. In the early 1960s tidal barriers were erected at Clarecastle and this has resulted in lowering water levels in Ennis during high tides. The barges had long since gone by that time and goods were transported by rail and road. Prior to the erection of the tidal barriers, flooding was commonplace in Ennis during most winters. Parnell Street, the Mill Road and the 'Post Office' field were regularly under water after a heavy downpour during the spring tides. Flooding has been almost completely eliminated, except for one quite exceptional downpour (the worst for a hundred years) on Tuesday and Wednesday, 5 and 6 August 1986. Once again the residents of Ennis witnessed flooding as in the days of old, with Parnell Street, the Mill Road and the 'Post Office' field awash with water.

Another interesting commercial activity of recent times was the arrival of cargo boats in the little harbour of Clarecastle. They carried coal and timber to the merchants of Ennis. It was the custom, even into the 1950s, to haul the coal from Clarecastle to Ennis with massive Shire horses pulling large high-walled carts. As they struggled to make it up the hill leading in to Ennis, their colleagues with empty carts were whipping their horses and achieving a good gait-o'going on the opposite side as they coasted downhill for another load. Of course, the hauliers were paid according to the amount of loads transported per day. It is known that a number of families had part of their winter fuel requirements furnished from the spillages at Clarecastle docks, and more from collecting lumps of coal which regularly fell from the carts as they lumbered over the bumpy surfaces on the way to Ennis.

Right into the early 1970s, the old Union Workhouse in Ennis was still in use as a hospital for the sick, the destitute and the old. Even at that time the remnants of the famine, the landless and the homeless were there to be seen in the form of old and sick men. Dressed in suits of rough wool, with similarly woven caps, leaning languidly against the workhouse walls they spent their days smoking plug tobacco in their clay pipes. It was pleasurable indeed to witness a heavy metal ball, dangling from a towering crane, demolish the entire 'County Home' in a matter of days. The end of pauperism and the genuflecting peasant was at hand. A well-designed modern hospital, St Joseph's, was erected in its place.

Ennis has been fortunate in recent times in securing a number of industries which are giving good employment. The first factory of note to make its appearance in the town was Braids Ltd. This firm was set up by an English company just before the Second World War and it has been manufacturing braids and shoe laces ever since. It gave employment to hundreds during the lean years of the 1940s and 1950s.

With the advent of industrialisation in the 1960s and 1970s, at least seven major foreign firms set up companies in Ennis, each giving employment in excess of one hundred people. In addition there are more than twenty lesser size firms employing an average of twenty-five people each. Some of these were started by local people.

As if to copperfasten the recent affluence in the county another important project which was started in the early 1980s recently came on stream, i.e. the ESB generating station at Moneypoint. This site, about five miles from Kilrush on the Shannon estuary, was selected by the ESB as being the best location in the country for its biggest coal-burning station. The turbines are powered by huge quantities of coal which are brought into the deep waters of the Shannon estuary in bulk tankers from abroad. The station will have a full capacity of 900 mW in three units of 300 mW each. The first unit was started up during

Moneypoint under construction, 1984.

1985 and it is expected that the station will be operating at full capacity by the end of 1987. Like the first generating station at Ardnacrusha, Moneypoint has brought much needed employment to its immediate area. The station which cost £730 million to build has a major consequence for Clare — the wage packets of its two hundred workers will mean an annual injection of over two million pounds into the local economy. It is a form of progress which in itself generates further confidence in the people for their future in the old kingdom of Thomond.

Clare in its long and troubled history has seen Stone Age Man, and man advancing through the Bronze and Iron Ages. She has witnessed tribes which produced many Munster and All-Ireland High Kings. Her fortunes were redirected by the Christian influence and by the love of learning. The county has been attacked many times, and has repulsed those attacks nearly as often. Internal warfare, coupled with a primitive social system, have for long periods utterly retarded her progress. Invasion, disorganisation and defeat have brought the county to her knees. She has been savagely depopulated by systematic transportation of the population and by lingering famine. Yet when native power was resumed, Clare as an integral part of a free country emerged from appalling poverty, to take her place amongst the developed countries of the world.

Majestic Dromoland Castle. Former home of the O'Brien dynasty and Lord Inchiquin. Now a luxury hotel.

The narrative of Clare's history must now pause here, and indeed it is at a much happier position than the Rev P. White found it at the conclusion of his own very thorough *History of Clare and the Dalcassian Clans.* His concluding chapter is worth recording here:

> This history of Clare now comes to an end. It shall not deal with the deplorable division caused in the National ranks by the unhappy fall of Mr Parnell. This is for wider ground than is taken up here, and may well be reserved for a calmer atmosphere. While the last lines are being written, Mr Gladstone is for the second time energetically pressing through Parliament a Home Rule Bill which in substance meets with the approval of all Irish Nationalists. If it gives to Ireland, as it must give sooner or later, self-government, the writer fondly hopes that whoever may in the future take up the thread of Clare narrative will find in it a subject more encouraging and more inspiring than fell to his lot.

How the wheel has turned! Clare has its freedom, its right of self determination within a country that has gained independence in part from the malevolent officiousness of England.

It is now the task of the majority of its inhabitants to improve their personal positions and to continue the recently begun process; to enjoy the freedom which was desired and dreamed of, fought, suffered and hungered for, and even died for, by countless thousands of their illustrious and daring ancestors since the very formation of these lands.

Appendix

Famous Clare Personalities

The most important person, as far as the people of the county were concerned, was undoubtedly the recognised leader of the most powerful clan. In the case of Clare this has always been a Dalcassian and after Brian Boru, an O'Brien.

An attempt was made here to form a list from earliest times up until the time such type of rule fell into disuse. As this list is compiled from various sources, and as far as is known, such a compilation has not been made elsewhere there may be some small variations with other records. Dates given are the dates when the individuals came to prominence — not always birth or death dates. As can be imagined all dates prior to AD 1000 are very approximate.

560 BC — 300 BC (est.) EBER
Son of Mil (of the Milesians). Celtic ancestor to all Munster and Clare (Thomond) kings.

AD 130 — 167 MOGHA OF THE SILVER HAND
Munster king and a descendant of Eber. Ruler of the southern half of Ireland (Leath Mogha — Mogha's Half). Slain at Moylena, AD 167.

AD 167 — 234 OILIOLL OLUIM
Only son of Mogha of the Silver Hand and father of all the men from whom the Dalcassians are descended. First king of Munster.

AD 234 — 245 AD Approx. FIACHA MUILLEATHAN
Grandson of Oilioll Oluim, and his successor as king of all Munster.

AD 240 — 280 Approx. CORMAC CAS
Second son of Oilioll Oluim. Ancestor to the Thomond O'Briens. Married a daughter of Oisin (of the Fianna). First King to be assigned to North Munster.

AD 265 Approx. MOGH CORB
Son of Cormac Cas. Munster King.

AD 315 Approx. LUIGHAIDH MEANN
Fourth descendant of Cormac Cas. Claimed Thomond (Clare) for his own.

AD 325 — 335 Approx. CONAL OF THE FLEET STEEDS
Son of Luighaidh Meann. Succeeded his father as King of Thomond.

AD 330 — 350 Approx. CAS
Son of Conal of the Fleet Steeds. The name 'Dalcassian' is derived from him. Seventh in descent from Cormac Cas and ancestor to all the important Clare clans. He had twelve sons.

AD 360 Approx. BLOD
Eldest son of Cas and direct ancestor of the O'Briens, McMahons, Malones, Moloneys, O'Currys, Hurleys, Reidy, Sexton, Hogans etc.

AD 360 Approx. CAISIN
Second son of Cas and direct ancestor of the MacNamaras, O'Gradys, McClancys, O'Deas, McInerneys, Meehans etc.

AD 365 Approx. CRIMTHAN (pronounced CRIFFAUN)
Sixth in descent from Oilioll Oluim. King of Munster, and of Ireland after AD 365.

AD 366 CONAL EACHLUAITH
King of Munster

(Between this period and the AD900s the strength of the south Munster clans — the Eoghanachts — overshadowed the Dalcassians. It appears they probably consolidated their position in Thomond while at the same time contested their position as kings of Munster. When hostilities began in Thomond against the Norse we find that monarchs and their exploits are again remembered).

AD 900 LORCAN
The Dalcassian King, and direct descendant of Oilioll Oluim.

AD 930 CENNÉDIG (KENNEDY)
A descendant of Oilioll Oluim and son of Lorcan. Father of Mahon and of Brian Boru. King of the Dalcassians.

AD 954 LACHTNA
King of North Munster. Uncle of Brian Boru.

AD 964 — 975 MAHON
Oldest son of Cennédig. Dalcassian king and Munster king.

AD 975 — 1014 BRIAN BORU (BOROIMHE)
Named Brian of the Tributes. Dalcassian king, King of Munster and High King of All Ireland. Fought the Danes and banished them from Ireland. Encouraged the use of surnames (eg. O'Brian). Most famous Dalcassian of all time.

1014 — 1028 TAIGH & DONOGH

Both sons of Brian Boru. Disputed the Dalcassian and Munster kingship between them after the death of their father at the battle of Clontarf.

1028 — 1064 DONOGH

Killed his brother Taigh and ruled Munster. Recognised as High King of Ireland in 1049.

1064 — 1086 TURLOGH

Dalcassian and Munster king. High King of All Ireland with opposition in 1075.

1086 — 1119 MURTAGH MORE O'BRIEN

Dalcassian, Munster and All-Ireland King. He was the last Dalcassian to achieve the Ard Righ's office.

1119 — 1142 CONOR-NA-CATHARACH

Son of Murtagh and brother of Turlogh O'Brien. Munster king.

1142 — 1167 TURLOGH O'BRIEN

Brother of Conor. Took over the principality of West Thomond. Contested the Munster kingship and died in that office in 1167.

During this period the principality was disputed between:-
TEIGUE GLE. — Prince of Thomond. Brother of Turlogh.
RORY O'BRIEN. — Prince of Thomond. Son of Turlogh.
CONOR (Son of Donal of Lismore) — Prince of Thomond.

1167 — 1168 MURTAGH O'BRIEN

Eldest son of Turlogh. Dalcassian King, killed by his cousin in 1168.

1168 — 1194 DONAL MORE O'BRIEN

Brother of Murtagh. Dalcassian and Munster King.

1194 — 1201 (Disputed)

During this period the kingship of the Dalcassians was disputed between:
Murtagh Dall - eldest son of Donal
Conor Roe - brother of Murtagh
Murtagh Finn - another brother.

1201 — 1242 DONOGH CAIRBREACH O'BRIEN

Prince of Thomond. Established new residence for the O'Briens at Clonroad Castle. Direct ancestor to the Kings and Earls of Thomond, and to the titled families of Inchiquin. He is also credited with having started work on the construction of Ennis Abbey, though it was not completed at the time of his death.

1242 — 1267 CONOR O'BRIEN

Son of Donogh. Prince of Thomond. Ennis Abbey was completed under his reign and the friars took occupancy. Known as Conor-Na-Suidaine.

1267 — 1277 BRIAN ROE O'BRIEN
Lord of Thomond. Died when drawn between horses in 1277.

1278 (only) DONOGH O'BRIEN
Son of Brian Roe. Ruled only West Thomond (West Clare) briefly.

1277 — 1306 TURLOGH O'BRIEN
Nephew of Brian Roe. He ruled in East Clare for a short time, and as such was considered Lord of Thomond. He is buried in the Abbey of Ennis.

1306 — 1311 DONOGH O'BRIEN
Lord of Thomond. He was a son of Turlogh. Slain by a kinsman in 1311.

1311 DERMOT O'BRIEN
Grandson of Brian Roe. Became Lord of Thomond when supported by the Norman, De Clare.

1311 — 1343 MURTAGH O'BRIEN
Lord of Thomond and a brother of Donogh. Recognized as true heir during this period.

1317 — 1350 BRIAN BAWN O'BRIEN
Prince of East Thomond until 1343 when he became Lord of Thomond in 1343 on the death of Murtagh.

1350 — 1355 DERMOT O'BRIEN
King of Thomond. Reigned without issue.

1355 — 1367 MAHON MOINMOY
King of Thomond and a nephew of Dermot. Won the seat by violence from Dermot.

1367 — 1369 TURLOGH MAOEL
Dispossessed by his nephew Brian.

1369 — 1399 BRIAN O'BRIEN
Recognised as Lord of Thomond. After 1377 he was called Brian Catha an Aenagh, having been successful in battle of Aenagh.

1399 — 1426 CONOR O'BRIEN
Lord of Thomond and a brother of Brian.

1426 — 1438 TEIGUE O'BRIEN
Lord of Thomond. A son of Brian Catha an Aenagh.

1438 — 1446 MAHON DALL O'BRIEN
Lord of Thomond. A brother of Teigue. Deposed in 1446.

1446 — 1459 TURLOGH O'BRIEN

Lord of Thomond. A younger brother of Teigue and Mahon. Known as Turlogh Bog (The Soft).

1459 — 1461 DONOGH

Son of Mahon Dall. Lord of Thomond.

1461 — 1466 TEIGUE AN CHOMHAID

King of Thomond and Munster, and contender for the Ard Righ. He was the eldest son of Turlogh.

1467 — 1496 CONOR NA SRONA

So named because of his large nose. He was a brother to Teigue. Barely recognised as Chief of the Dalcassians in the early part of his career. Finished very powerfully as Lord of Thomond.

1496 — 1499 TURLOGH OGE

Surnamed Gilla Dubh. He died after an inconspicuous reign in 1499.

1500 — 1528 TURLOGH DON O'BRIEN

Lord of Thomond. He was involved in many quarrels, yet was recognized for his nobility.

1528 — 1539 CONOR O'BRIEN

King of Thomond. Eldest son of Turlogh. Last of the descendants of Brian Boru as supreme ruler in Thomond.

1539 — 1551 MURROGH THE TANIST

Fifty-seventh and last king of Thomond when he was created the First Earl of Thomond by the English on 1 July 1542. First Baron Inchiquin.

1542 — 1553 DONOGH THE FAT

Created Baron of Ibricken by the English. Succeeded Murrough on his death (1551) as Prince of Thomond. By virtue of Henry VIII's patent the title of Second Earl of Thomond descended to him.

1550 — 1559 DONOGH O'BRIEN

Disputed the title of Earl with Donal and Conor. Restored briefly in Inchiquin.

1550 — 1559 TEIGUE O'BRIEN

Disputed the title of Earl with Donal and Conor. Restored briefly in Inchiquin.

1553 — 1579 SIR DONAL O'BRIEN

Recognized by his clansmen as true king. Founder of the Ennistymon O'Briens. When he died he was also the Tanist of Thomond. So ended the two thousand year old Brehon law practice of selecting the Prince of Thomond.

1553 — 1581 CONOR O'BRIEN
Disputed his position as Earl with the English — not recognised. Surrendered the ancient Dalcassians rights to the English. Restored as Third Earl of Thomond in 1571.

1581 — 1624 DONOGH O'BRIEN
Son of Conor, and Fourth Earl of Thomond.

1624 — 1639 HENRY O'BRIEN
Fifth Earl of Thomond.

1639 — 1657 BARNABUS
Sixth Earl of Thomond.

1657 — 1691 HENRY
Seventh Earl of Thomond. Governor of Co. Clare.

1691 — 1741 HENRY
Eighth Earl of Thomond. (Last of the line. Family now anglicised and residing in England.)

TITLES OF INCHIQUIN
(Murrogh the Tanist was the First Baron Inchiquin).

1551 — 1552 DERMOT
Second Baron Inchiquin.

1552 — 1573 MURROGH
Third Baron Inchiquin.

1573 — 1597 MURROGH
Fourth Baron Inchiquin.

1597 — 1624 DERMOT
Fifth Baron Inchiquin.

1624 — 1674 MURROGH AN TOTHAINE
Called Murrogh of the Burnings. He was Sixth Baron and First Earl of Inchiquin. Professional soldier, Governor of Catalonia and Majorca.

1674 — 1691 WILLIAM
Seventh Baron Inchiquin. Second Earl Inchiquin.

1691 — 1719 WILLIAM
Eighth Baron Inchiquin. Third Earl Inchiquin.

1719 — 1777 WILLIAM
Ninth Baron Inchiquin. Fourth Earl Inchiquin.

1777 — 1808 MURROGH
Tenth Baron Inchiquin. Fifth Earl Inchiquin.

1808 — 1846 WILLIAM
Eleventh Baron Inchiquin. Sixth Earl Inchiquin.

1846 — 1855 ADMIRAL LORD JAMES
Twelfth Baron Inchiquin. Seventh Earl Inchiquin. Because he had no children all of his titles, except Baron of Inchiquin, became extinct.

1855 — 1872 SIR LUCIUS O'BRIEN
His claim to the title of Thirteenth Baron of Inqhicuin was granted by the House of Lords in England in April 1862. Now the senior branch of the O'Briens. Referred to as 'the O'Brien of Thomond'.

From the Modern Era

JOHN O'CONNELL BIANCONI (1871 — 1929)

John O'Connell Bianconi lived at Ballylean near Kildysart in south Clare. On his large estate he demonstrated his talents in engineering and science by building and utilising many novel pieces of mechanical equipment. Some of the systems which he put into operation included a telephone network, an unusual railway circuit on his farm, and also an electric generator. It is said that he constructed a steam engine traction system which operated a regular service between Kildysart and Ennis. However, his farmyard railway was the most famous of his inventions and he used it to transport all his farm produce at harvest time. Another of his transport services included a regular shipping route between Limerick and Kilrush, which also served Kildysart and Labasheeda.

As well as being a Justice of the Peace he also served as High Sheriff in the county. He was noted for his generosity and for entertaining guests at gala picnics on his estate. After his death in October 1929, all of his unique equipment was disposed of by auction for very nominal sums.

SAMUEL HENRY BINDON (1812 — 1879)

Samuel Henry Bindon was a highly talented lawyer of the nineteenth century. He was born in County Clare in 1812 and he entered Trinity College where he received his BA in 1835. In 1838 he was called to the Irish Bar. Bindon's literary work included editing the works of Nicholas French in two volumes in Duffy's Library of Ireland series, 1846. He was also secretary to the Tenants League. Shortly afterwards he emigrated to Australia where he rose to a position of considerable distinction at the Australian Bar. He went on to become a famous judge and then Cabinet Minister in the administration of that country. He died in Australia in 1879.

JAMES BARTHOLOMEW BLACKWELL (1765 — 1825)

Born in Ennis in 1765, James Bartholomew Blackwell was later educated at the Lombardian College in Paris. He became attracted to the army and enlisted in the Esterhazy Regiment of Huzzars. When the French Revolution broke out Blackwell was deeply involved in the movemet towards political change. It is now believed that he led an assault on the Bastile itself during those heady days of the French Revolution.

He did not forget his homeland. He supported Wolfe Tone and Napper Tandy by sending military expeditions to Ireland with the hope of prising the English out of the country. The first expedition in 1896 was wrecked in a storm off Bantry Bay and the second in 1898 surrendered to British Naval forces off the Donegal coast. Blackwell was later captured and for his part in the operation received two years in Kilmainham Gaol.

He later returned to France where Napoleon placed him in charge of a Battalion in the Irish Regiment. A man of extraordinary adventure, it seems he took part in the disastrous Russian Campaign, surviving to tell the tale. James Blackwell next became military governor of La Petite Pierre in Lorraine, and in 1819 it is recorded that he was honoured as Brevet-Officer in the Royal Order of the Legion of Honour.

LIEUT. GEN. MICHAEL BRENNAN (1896 — 1986)

One of the latter day warring Dalcassians, Michael Brennan became famous as a freedom fighter and an outstanding officer of the Irish Army. He was born in Meelick in 1896 and at the age of sixteen he was already a leader of the Fianna boys in Limerick.

As an early member of the volunteers he made a significant contribution to the events which led to the historic Rising of Easter Week 1916. With his brothers Paddy and Austin he organised many of the guerrilla companies which fought the War of Independence in Clare. Brennan was jailed after the Rising but managed to escape from an English prison. He supported the Sinn Féin candidate in the 1917 East Clare by-election. Shortly afterwards he was re-captured and was subsequently in and out of jail until 1919. While in prison he supported many of the hunger-strike efforts to regain rights lost after the death of Thomas Ashe. Right up to the Truce of 11 July, 1921 he was a wanted man.

He organised Flying Columns against the RIC, and the Black and Tans. Brennan led the attack on the first police barracks to fall in the country, at Newmarket-on-Fergus. This remarkable soldier led many other daring raids during the duration of the 'Troubles'. In 1920 Michael Brennan was Chairman of the Sinn Féin monopolised Clare County Council. When the Treaty was signed in December 1921 he was one of the large number of councillors to support it.

He joined the new Irish army at its formation and went on to hold many distinguished posts. Ultimately, he became Chief of General Staff in 1931, a position he held for a record nine years until he retired from the army in 1940.

After his millitary career he worked in the Office of Public Works for a number of years until his final retirement. Michael Brennan, freedom fighter and soldier, died during the month of October in 1986. As befitting a man of such distinguished service to his country he was buried with full military honours in Dean's Grange Cemetery, Dublin.

SIR FREDERICK WILLIAM BURTON (1816 — 1900)

Frederick Burton was born in Corofin House in 1816. He was a gifted painter and gained membership of the R.I.A. in 1839. Between the years 1851 — 1858 he went on to advanced studies in Munich, West Germany. He became FSA in 1863 and LLD TCD, in 1896. This remarkable Clareman was next appointed Director of the National Gallery of London in 1874. He was renowned for his portraits of many distinguished Irishmen of his time. He went into retirement in 1894 and died in London in 1900.

WILLIAM CARROLL (1817 — 1889)

A successful builder and civil contractor who was born in Ennis in 1817. During a cholera outbreak in 1849 he moved his family to Ballybeg, Clarecastle. The house which he built there 'Abbey View' is still standing. This house remained in the family possession until 1976. His other commercial activities included a saw mill and two timber yards, one of which occupied the present site of the derelict Gaiety Cinema. Carroll built the 'Post Office' bridge over the Fergus at Bank Place as well as the old metal bridge at Doora which remained in use until 1974 when a new bridge was constructed. Some of the better known structures which he built would include the Franciscan Friary, completed in 1884, and the O'Connell Monument which was unveiled in 1865. He was buried in the family vault in Drumcliffe cemetery, a structure which he also built himself.

MICHAEL CUSACK (1847 — 1906)

Born in Carron, in the Barony of Burren, in the famine year of 1847. He became a local school teacher and was fluent in Irish from an early age. He had a great passion for all things Irish, games, dances and folklore. He regarded, not just his own district, but all of Ireland as his home. He went on to teach school in Enniscorthy and in Lough Cutra until 1871. Cusack later went to Dublin where he operated a 'grinding' school at Emmet Street. From his travels around the country he became aware of the declining interest in games and old traditions. He issued his famous circular to establish The Gaelic Athletic Association in 1884. The GAA went on to become the biggest and best known organisation in the country. The quality of the games have reached international standards. Prior to organising the GAA he showed a distinct interest in rugby and cricket, being a useful rugby player himself first with Cusack's Academy XV and later with the Phoenix Rugby Club. Perhaps it was the organisation of those sports that inspired him (for inspired he became) to organise the fading Irish games in the same way. After 1882 he became obsessed with the idea of national games. He met P.W. Nally in Dublin and both showed great concern at the general disorganised state of Irish athletics. Cusack is credited with reviving Dublin hurling in the 1880s. Michael Cusack died on a Dublin street in 1906.

WILLIE CLANCY (1918 — 1972)

A son of Gilbert Clancy (flute, concertina and pipe player), Willie Clancy was one of the best known musicians of the modern era. From an early age he was steeped in the traditional culture of Irish music. He was born in Miltown Malbay on 24 December, 1918. He played his first tin whistle at five years. Greatly influenced by his grandmother, who had a keen ear for music, by his father and by Garrett Barry the celebrated blind piper, Willie Clancy went on to master the pipes himself. When Martin Talty caught him playing a tune in his classroom, a friendship was struck up which lasted for a lifetime. Both played concert flutes at every available dance, wake and wedding to perfect their craft. In between he won an Oireachtas medal for the tin whistle in 1947.

Having trained as a carpenter he was unable to find profitable work locally, so he emigrated to London. While there he continued with the Irish music, rubbing shoulders with such notable players as Johnny Doran and Seamus Ennis. He returned from London in 1957 after a three year stay. He married Doirin Healy and resettled in Miltown Malbay. From 1957 until 1972 the summer music sessions in the west Clare town became widely renowned with Willie Clancy as one of the main attractions. Pipe-making, reed-making and all things connected with the instrument were explored and advanced by the Clancy influence. He gave many performances on both radio and televison as well as live sessions in his local area.

THOMAS DERMODY (1775 — 1802)
A renowned writer and romantic poet, Thomas Dermody child prodigy, was born in Ennis in 1775. His father ran a school in Ennis and in order to offset costs he pressed the younger Dermody into service as a teacher of Latin and Greek. Dermody's mother and younger brother died about this time and Dermody's response was to write a commemorative poem in their honour. Shortly afterwards he left for Dublin where he became enchanted with the bookshops and the literary way of life. Unfortuately he had been addicted to drink at an early age and this marred his output and his way of life.

One of his better known accomplishments at that time was a critique he wrote on the contrasting styles of Milton and Shakespeare. It received very wide acclaim. Shortly after this he left for London, against his patron's advice, where he lived in very trying conditions. He lived in poverty and depravation and was forced to turn to the commercial practice of writing soliciting letters to earn his keep. He joined the army and went to Flanders where he gave a good account of himself. On his return to London he reverted to his old ways and lived in inhuman conditions in a broken down hovel where he died at the very young age of twenty-seven years. He was buried at Lewisham.

BIDDY EARLY (1798 — 1874)
She was baptised Bridget Ellen Connors, but always went by her mother's name, Early. Her mother was a noted herbalist and passed on her secrets and potions to her young daughter when she died. Biddy was only sixteen at the time.

Young Biddy was a striking child of long red hair and green-blue eyes. She was said to be constantly conversing with the fairies when she was alone, and because of this the locals were initially sceptical of her. When her father died she went travelling the roads of Clare. She became a domestic in Carheen and was evicted by landlord Sheehy. When she put a curse on him he was later murdered by his infuriated tenants, a fact which gave rise to her prophetic ability. In her early twenties she married a widower named Pat Molloy who was twice her age. The union produced a son, Paddy, but Biddy became a widower at twenty-five. Shortly afterwards she married her stepson, John Molloy.

By this time she had become very famous for her cures and predictions. It is said that Daniel O'Connell once visited her for advice. In 1840 her second husband died from a liver ailment and she then married a young man from

Quin, called Tom Flannery. They moved to a two-roomed cottage overlooking the lake at Kilbarron. To complement the many potions she already had, her son Paddy received a special bottle from the fairies having assisted one of their clans in a midnight hurling match! Her cures and predictions drew very large crowds which eventually brought the wrath of the clergy down on her. In 1856 she was charged with practising witchcraft but was dismissed for lack of evidence — nobody would testify against her.

Biddy married her fourth husband on 27 July 1869 in Limerick. He died from over-drinking a year later when Biddy was seventy-two years old. In 1874 she fell ill and was attended by the local priest, Fr Connellan. It is thought that he gained some measure of repentance from her for he threw her magic bottle into Kilbarron lake. Her funeral was attended by twenty-seven priests and yet she was buried in an unmarked grave. Just a few years ago, RTE were about to screen a TV documentary on her life when the transmitting equipment blacked out due to technical problems. Perhaps Biddy still has the power!

BISHOP JOHN GREGG (1798 — 1878)
Born just outside Ennis at Barefield, he attended a local school under Stephen O'Halloran in Ennis. He went on to further education at Trinity College, Dublin, where he took his MA in 1825. He was ordained in 1836 in the Church of Ireland and served in Bethesda Chapel (1836); Trinity Church (1839—62); and as the Archdeacon of Kildare (1857). When he was consecrated Bishop of Cork, Cloyne and Ross in 1862 he commissioned William Burgess to design St Fin Barre's Cathedral there. The building was erected during his episcopacy. He was succeeded by his son Robert Samuel. He is honoured by a memorial window in Drumcliffe Parish Church, Ennis.

WILLIAM VESEY-FITZGERALD (1783 — 1843)
A landowner and politician (Conservative) who was born in Ennis. After his education at Oxford he went in to local politics. He was MP for Ennis at Westminister from 1808 to 1812; again from 1813 to 1818. He was also returned for the period 1831-1832. He represented Clare county during 1818 to 1828. Fitzgerald became Lord of the Irish Treasury and a Privy Councillor in 1810. In 1810 he was an English Privy Councillor and from 1820 until 1823 he was Envoy Extraordinary to Sweden. This man was always a popular Catholic landlord even though O'Connell defeated him in one election contest. Another seat was found for him in Cornwall. Having been re-elected for Ennis in 1831 he was made President of the Board of Trade and served there from 1841 to 1843.

PATRICK HILLERY (1923 —   )
This man from Miltown Malbay is a doctor, politician and President of Ireland. He was educated in the local national school and then at Rockwell College. He went on to UCD where he took his MD in 1947. In 1951 he was elected TD for West Clare on behalf of the Fianna Fáil party. He represented that constituency until 1973. Patrick Hillery served Fianna Fáil governments in various ministeries as follows:— Minister for Education 1959-65 : Industry & Commerce 1965-66 : Labour 1966-69 : External Affairs 1962-72. As Minister for

External Affairs he conducted negotiations on behalf of Ireland's entry into the EEC in 1973. He then left Irish politics to become Irish Commissioner at the EEC with responsibility for Social Affairs (1973-76). When President Cearbhall Ó Dálaigh resigned from office Patrick Hillery became the agreed candidate for all the parties and he was duly elected in November 1976. He is currently in his second term of office and continues to represent his county and country with distinction.

JOHN P. HOLLAND (1841 — 1914)
John Holland must be given credit for inventing the first underwater boat — the submarine. In Liscannor, where he was born, in 1841, it is said that he first got the idea for an underwater boat when looking out on Liscannor Bay. His father, who was a coast guard, died when he was quite young and he was sent to the CBS in Limerick. He joined that congregation in 1858 and became a teacher. He taught in various centres in Ireland but even at that stage he had some basic plans made for his underwater boat. A science teacher in Cork also gave him encouragement and advice. He was forced to leave the Christian Brothers due to ill health, and he emigrated to America. He spent many years in America building and perfecting his invention but was frustrated by the US Navy who were sceptical about his device because they found it difficult to use. Finally, the Fenians in America decided to finance him. At last, he went under the Passiac river in a test boat, *The Fenian Ram* for a considerable period, proving that the concept worked. The British and American navies finally came round to his way of thinking. He sold his first submarine, *The Holland,* to the British Navy and this was launched on 2 October, 1901, in Barrow-on-Furness, England. Holland lost control of John Holland Torpedo Boat Company which he founded, and it is now part of the world renowned Dynamics Corporation of Grotton, Connecticut, USA. John Philip Holland died in 1914, having received very little for his invention in the way of either money or recognition.

PAT KIRBY (1936 —   )
The ancient Irish sport of handball has been mastered to the highest international standards by a truly great Dalcassian sportsman, Pat Kirby. Born in Tuamgraney in east Clare, this remarkable sportsman excelled at hurling and handball from an early age. Kirby played hurling for both Ennis and Clare before emigrating to the USA in 1959. While at home he won many Irish titles in the courts and often seemed unbeatable. He won the world's single crown in 1970, representing the USA, having already won their senior championship. He won a Master's double title with Matt Purcell (Kildare) and the Master's singles in Dublin in 1984. In 1986 he won the World championship in Canada, as well as retaining the Masters (over 40) singles and doubles. And all this at fifty years of age! In June of 1986 he took his sixth US Masters Championship which prompted the Americans to include him in their Hall of Fame — the first non-American player to be so honoured. Still living in the USA and playing handball, this highly talented sportsman must be considered one of the greatest sportsmen that graced any code, anywhere in the world.

SIR ROBERT MICHAEL LAFFAN (1821 — 1882)

Born in Skehana, Co. Clare, Robert Laffan went to France at an early age where he was educated first at the French College of Pont Levoy and later at the Royal Military College at Woolwich. He saw service in South Africa, Mauritius, Malta and Ceylon. Sir Robert became a respected authority on army engineering and he was sent to examine and report on the famous Suez Canal. He was there to witness the opening of the canal in 1869. He is also responsible for completely laying out the barracks and manoeuvring plains at Aldershot — they were renamed in his honour as 'Laffan's Plain'.

Having been a commander in Gibralter he went on to become Commander-in-Chief of the Bermudas, where he was promoted to Brigadier-General. It was while there he was knighted and became recognised as Governor of Bermuda. He died there in 1882. Robert Laffan was buried in Bermuda with full military honours having lain in state for two days.

DONNACHADH RUADH MacCONMARA (1715 — 1810)

Donnachadh Ruadh was a poet and reconteur who was born at Cratloe in 1715. He spent some years in the Irish College in Rome where he studied for the priesthood. When he discovered that he was unsuitable for the religious life he returned to Ireland and lived in Waterford for a time.

While in Waterford he became famous as a poet and a singer of poetic songs in many of the seamen's taverns in that city. From there he emigrated to Newfoundland where he continued his entertaining in the taverns. He also developed his writing in Gaelic poetry. Some of his better known compositions include *The Adventures of a Luckless Fellow* and *As I was Walking one Evening Fair*. Perhaps, Gaelic scholars would be in disagreement as to the quality of his work, maintaining that he was careless and more concerned with popularising his compositions. He did, nevertheless, produce some epic poems and he was one of the few classical lyrists during the impoverished years prior to the great famine.

ANDREW MacCURTIN (? — 1749)

MacCurtin came from a long line of poets, and was always a strict disciplinarian in the traditional method of rhyming. Born at Moyglass, Kilmurry Ibricken, he soon succeeded to the hereditary title of Ollamh to the O'Briens of Thomond. Many of his manuscripts are preserved in Trinity College, the Royal Irish Academy and the British Museum and some are in private hands. Eugene O'Curry considered him to be one of the best Gaelic scholars of his day. He sold much of his property to finance his travel and learning. He eventually opened a poetry school in his native parish in order to earn a living (having deserted his patrons, the O'Briens, in a fit of pique). When he died in 1749 he was buried in an unmarked grave in the church of Kilfarboy.

FIREBALL MacNAMARA (? — 1836)

His correct name was John MacNamara, but dubbed 'Fireball MacNamara' on account of his propensity for fighting duels, most of which ended fatally for his opponents. He was born in Clare towards the end of the eighteenth century, of Moyreisk father, John MacNamara, who was MP for Clare in 1790.

Fireball spent much of his time at sport and leisure and many a legend quickly sprung up about his activities. Michael Hogan, Bard of Thomond, wrote two poems in his honour: 'The grave of Sean Buidhe MacNamara' and 'Fireball MacNamara's address to his pistols'.

MacNamara claimed to have been wounded in the battle of Vinegar Hill in Wexford. It is known that he fought at least forty-five duels and acted as second in many more. He gave a special name to his pistols, Bás gan Sagart (Death without a priest in attendance). He was the last of the Moyreisk Mac-Namaras, the last of the fire-eating Irish petty chieftains, his wild life being responsible for squandering his entire estate. Fireball MacNamara is buried in Quin Abbey where even his poet, Michael Hogan, recognised his life of folly when he wrote in part: 'Where are the honours you have won?' With the death of this MacNamara went one of the last outrageous Dalcassians in the old spirit of things.

STEPHEN JOSEPH MEANY (1822 — 1888)
Born in Newhall, about three miles from Ennis, he received an early education in the district. Although he published some verse and pamphlets, he was primarily famous for being a journalist and newspaper editor of some ability. He was first a reporter with the *Limerick Chronicle* and shortly afterwards went to Dublin to work for the *Daily Freeman* in the same capacity. It was not long before he was running two papers, *The Irish Tribune,* and the *Irish Felon.* Those publications were outspoken against the English administration and his views got him into hot water with the authorities. He was detained in Castlefergus Castle for one year by the authorities. On his release he resumed as editor of the *Limerick and Clare Examiner.*

Later he left Ireland and went to reside in America. He became editor of a number of publications there and settled in Toledo City where he made many friends including the famous General Shearman. On a subsequent visit to England he was arrested and imprisoned by the government. He served two years of a fifteen year sentence in Mountjoy Prison and was eventually released under pressure from the American Government. He returned to edit the *Evening Democrat* in Waterbury, Connecticut, where he died in 1888.

BRIAN MERRIMAN (1747 — 1805)
Merriman was born in Clare in or around the year 1747. The exact location of his birth is uncertain and has been given variously as Ennis, Ennistymon, Cranny and Clondegad. He is most associated with Feakle where he taught school for twenty years. He married locally and two girls were born of the marriage. He is best known for his famous poem 'Cuirt an Mhean Oiche' ('The Midnight Court') which has been translated into English by many translators.

In commemoration of Merriman's poetic works an Annual Merriman Summer School is held each year in the county. In Feakle churchyard there is a plaque honouring his memory. Brian Merriman, the last of the great Gaelic scholars and poets, moved to Limerick later in life where he taught mathematics. He died in Limerick on 27 July 1805.

WILLIAM MULREADY, RA (1786 — 1863)

A noted painter who was born in Ennis in 1786. His works included landscapes, rural, and homely scenes in which he displayed an unusual talent in presenting detail and in capturing the essence of the quieter scenes of his day. Such was his talent that he was elected to the Royal Academy School at the very young age of thirty — an outstanding achievement. His output was low, probably evidence of his meticulous attention to detail — he often produced a number of sketches before committing himself to canvas.

The Queen of England purchased some of his work for the Royal Collection at an exhibition which was held in Gore House, London, in 1853. Again, in 1972 a major exhibition of his drawings was staged in the Victoria and Albert Museum, when some of his best works were seen. The bi-centenary of his birth was commemorated with an exhibition in the De Valera Library, Ennis, in 1986.

CATHERINE AMELIA O'BRIEN (1881 — 1963)

Catherine Amelia O'Brien was a highly talented artist who worked in stain glass. She was born at Durra House, near Spancilhill. Her father was Pierce O'Brien, a man of property and a Justice of the Peace for Clare. Her work includes a memorial in stain glass to her parents which may be seen in Drumcliffe Parish Church, Bindon Street, Ennis. She also extended her skills to the craft of *opus sectile* (inserting coloured glass into concrete frames) and an example of this section of her work is in the Franciscan Friary of Athlone. She advanced her skills by further study under A E Child and William Orpen, and by working in the Tower Glass Studios producing work for home and abroad. Further examples of her creations are in the Church of Ireland, Killoughter, Co. Cavan ('The Sower'). The Church of Ireland in Harold's Cross, Dublin, carries the 'Good Samaritan' and there are two windows displaying her talents in the Church of Ireland, Gorey, Co. Wexford. She and her colleagues in the studio raised the art of working in stained glass to a new level. One of the commissions she was working on when she died was a window for Aras an Uachtarain, Dublin. It was finished by her companions in the studio. To commemorate her death and her life's work, her brother, Pierce O'Brien commissioned a window from Patrick Pollen for the St Lawrence O'Toole Chapel of Christ Church, Dublin.

CHARLOTTE GRACE O'BRIEN (1845 — 1909)

Primarily noted as an author, but she also took an active part in politics and social work. She was born in Cahirmoyle in 1845, a daugther of Smith O'Brien. She spent much of her childhood abroad with her father. When she returned to Ireland she became involved in the plight of emigrants, urging better accommodation and helping in whatever way she could. She started a beneficiary scheme for the peasantry. Her writing consisted of lyrical poems and a particularly clever novel called 'Light and Shade', which she wrote in 1878. She was a staunch advocate of the Gaelic League. When she died in 1909 Stephen Gwynn, wrote a memoir of her life.

MATHEW O'BRIEN (1814 — 1855)

Son of Mathew O'Brien, a doctor who had a good practice in Ennis, the younger Mathew became an astronomer and a mathematician. He went on to Cambridge where he received his MA in 1841. He was awarded the Moderatorship of Mathematics in 1843. His next appointment was as Professor of Natural Philosophy and Astronomy, King's College, London, in 1844. Author of many mathematical works including 'Differential Calculus' (1842); 'Plane Co-ordinate Geometry' (1844); and a 'Treatise on Mathematical Geography' (1852). In addition he issued many pamphlets on mathematical subjects. He was sent to the Channel Islands for health reasons but regrettably he died there on 23 August 1855.

EDNA O'BRIEN (1932 —   )

Edna O'Brien is Clare's most famous living writer. She was born at Tuamgraney and brought up in a devoutly Catholic family. Her further attendance at Catholic schools probably influenced her as a writer. She has written many successful novels and volumes of short stories, some of which have been the subjects for films. She left Clare having completed her schooling and went to live in Dublin and later London, where she is currently residing.

FRANCES MARCELLA O'BRIEN (1840 — 1883)

She was born at Peafield near Ennis on 24 June 1840. Her mother, Marcella, died at thirty years of age. William, her father, emigrated with the older children leaving Attie, (as Frances Marcella became affectionately known) behind in Newgrove with her grandmother. Attie was always delicate as a child when she suffered from asthma, and perhaps because of this she took a deep interest in books. At a comparatively young age she developed into a very accomplished poet and novelist. She regularly contributed stories to the *Irish Monthly* and poems to many other periodicals, all of which were of very high standard. She travelled to Dublin in March of 1873, but the rigours of the journey had an adverse effect on her. Her untimely death in Dublin, on 5 April 1883, undoubtedly robbed us of many more quality works. She is buried in the old-churchyard of Killadysert.

WILLIAM SMITH O'BRIEN (1803 — 1864)

Smith O'Brien was a noted Young Irelander who was born at Dromoland in 1803. He received a first class education at both Harrow and Cambridge. He was elected MP in Ennis in 1828. He was a great advocate of supporting the poor and he also urged the payment of the Catholic clergy. He joined the Repeal Association in 1843 and he also helped found the Irish Confederation in 1847. When he urged formation of a 'National Guard' in 1848 he got into real trouble with the authorities. At his trial the jury failed to agree and when he was released he started to 'raise the country'. A reward was offered for his arrest, and this was met with little support from the populus at large. An attack by him on widow McCormack's house at Boulah Common brought the wrath of the police on him once again. He was arrested and sent to Clonmel for trial. The jury found him guilty of high treason and he was sentenced to death, but this was later commuted to penal servitude for life and he was transported to Tasmania. He was released in 1854 and unconditionally pardoned in 1856. After this he returned home and took no further part in politics. In 1864 he died in Bangor in Wales.

EUGENE O'CAHAN (1600 — 1650 Approx.)

Born of noble parents in the beginning of the seventeenth century, Eugene O'Cahan went on to become a Franciscan priest. At sixteen years he entered the Order of St Francis and later went to Rome where he was ordained in 1622.

While abroad his brilliance in theology enabled him to defend public theses in the years between 1635 and 1639. During that particular period he also taught philosophy at Boretta in northern Italy.

He returned to Ireland in 1641. In 1644 he opened a public school at Quin. Such was the reputation of the school that it contained up to eight hundred students from all over Ireland, including nineteen of the O'Broudin family (famous Clare historians). Eugene O'Cahan was Guardian of Ennis Friary between 1644/1645 — 1647 and he was also Lector in 1647. He was transferred to County Limerick in 1648. While travelling on a mission through north Cork he was captured by the Puritans who immediately strangled him without mercy. His case has been put to Rome for recognition as a martyr.

PETER O'CONNELL (1775 — 1826)

Peter O'Connell was a renowned scholar who was born at Carne (Moneypoint) in 1775. He organised a school there for the study of Gaelic Literature. O'Connell collected much material locally for a great Irish-English dictionary. When he was unable to obtain patronage to keep up his studies he was forced to sell his manuscripts in Tralee for a few paltry shillings. The manuscripts were subsequently redeemed by Eugene O'Curry and are now stored in the British Museum. Some sources claim that Peter O'Connell was the best Irish scholar in the country over a century ago. He is buried in the same grave as the Coleen Bawn, in Burrane Cemetery.

EUGENE O'CURRY (1794 — 1862)

He was born at Dunaha, near Carrigaholt, in west Clare. A self-educated man who managed to become accomplished in reading and writing in both the Irish and English languages, he developed a unique ability to translate from the early Gaelic manuscripts. It is likely that he learned much of this skill from his father, Owen Mór O'Curry, who had an immense knowledge of every old legend and tradition in Thomond. As a young man he taught school for five years at Kilferagh, near Kilkee. Then he moved to the city of Limerick in 1824 where he is reputed to have held a number of jobs, including one as a labourer on the building of Thomond Bridge and as warder in Limerick lunatic asylum.

However, his beloved studies could not be neglected and he returned to them in the service of George Pertie's Department, where he was employed in the elucidation of old Irish place names. O'Curry became widely respected for his deep fund of knowledge in deciphering obtruse passages in old manuscripts. In recognition for his work he was appointed Professor of Irish Archaeology and History at the University of Ireland by its first rector, John Henry Newman.

O'Curry's greatest work was the translation of the Brehon Laws. When they were published there was no acknowledgement of his contribution to the work. He translated such works as; 'The Tain Bo', 'The Vision of Adamnan', 'The Origin and history of the Boromean Tribute', 'The Vision of Mac-Coinglinne and the Festology of Aengus'. His searches in the British Museum uncovered the most important and long-lost *Tripartite Life of St Patrick.* Eugene O'Curry died suddenly on 30 July 1862, and he was buried in Glasnevin Cemetery, Dublin.

THE O'GORMAN MAHON (1800 — 1891)
Correct name was James Patrick Mahon. Adopted the title 'The O'Gorman Mahon' to incorporate his mother's name and woe betide the man who failed to respect it! Born in Mill Street, Ennis, he came into much property at an early age, his father being a merchant in the town. He received his BA from TCD in 1822. The O'Gorman Mahon supported O'Connell in the election of 1829. He was elected MP for Ennis in 1830 having unseated O'Connell and quarrelled with him. Before going abroad he was called to the Bar in 1834. He led a cavalier life fighting in both hemispheres under many flags. When he returned he was re-elected MP for Ennis in 1879. One of the last of the old dare-devil Irishmen. Died in Chelsea in 1891.

THOMAS O'GORMAN (1725 — 1809)
Known as 'The Chevalier' because he was created chevalier by Louis XV of France. In addition he married the sister of Chevalier D'Eon and received large vineyards as his dowry.

Thomas O'Gorman was born at Kilmihil sometime around 1725. His extremely tall structure of six feet five inches made him an oustanding soldier in the Irish Brigade. King Louis was very impressed by his commanding size which was why he made him chevalier. O'Gorman began a wine trade between France and Ireland which soon flourished, and he frequently visited Ireland during that time. He subsequently became interested in Irish genealogy and soon was making a good profit from importing pedigrees to the continent. He procured pedigrees for many descendants of the 'Wild Geese', one such family history which he compiled was that of Count O'Reilly, General-in-Chief of the Spanish Army.

With the advent of the French Revolution, 'The Chevalier's' property was confiscated and he was obliged to return to Dublin where he lived for many years in poverty. Unable to recover his former position, in spite of having three sons in His Majesty's Army, finally, he returned to Clare and spent his last days at Dromellihy. He died on 18 November 1809, and he was buried in the church yard of Kilmacduane.

BRIAN O'LOONEY (1828 — 1901)
Brian O'Looney was another noted Gaelic scholar. Born in the parish of Inagh, where he attended the local hedge school under bardic tutor Seamus Mac-Cruitin. This experience instilled in him a love for manuscripts and things historical.

Being patriotic, he became involved in an insurrection staged by William

Smith O'Brien at Ballingarry, Co Tipperary. This little rising was more symbolic than anything else but it did get him into hot water with the authorities. He escaped to Limerick city where he managed to obtain passage on a ship sailing for America. Some years later he returned to Ireland after the incident had been forgotten.

He renewed his acquaintance with Smith O'Brien who was residing in Brussels at the time. Smith O'Brien introduced him to the work of cataloguing Irish papers. This led to his appointment (in succession to Eugene O'Curry) as Professor of Irish Language, Literature and Celtic Archaeology at the Catholic University in Dublin. Later he founded the Society for the Preservation of the Irish Language.

O'Looney is best known for his translations of the Clare poets Ó Cormin, MacCruitin and Ó hUiginn. He also completed an extensive study on the importance of the ancient ruins on Mount Callan. As a result of his findings traditional worship at the Mount Callan site was later transferred to St Muchan's holy well, Ennistymon.

Brian O'Looney died in Killiney, Co. Dublin, in 1901.

BRENDAN O'REGAN (1917 —   )

He was born in Sixmilebridge in 1917. His early training was in the hotel business, his family being owners of the famous Old Ground Hotel in Ennis. When he was a young man he went to France, Switzerland and Germany to study hotel management. His first position was manager of the Falls Hotel in Ennistymon.

At the age of twenty-five he was appointed first comptroller of the international airport for flying boats at Foynes, Co Limerick. When flying operations were switched to Rineanna, Co Clare, O'Regan took control there. He set up the now-famous duty free shop in the airport — the first of its kind anywhere in the world. He became the first chief executive of SFADCo and in 1958 he was appointed Chairman of Bord Failte. International recognition came his way in 1977 when he was elected to the travel Hall of Fame in Madrid. Since his retirement from public life he has turned his attentions to the problems of Northern Ireland and once again has come up with an 'O'Regan' solution — the setting up of a North-South co-operative movement. The objective of this organisation is to break down the barriers of hatred between the communities in an effort to pave the way towards lasting peace. O'Regan must be regarded as one of the most effective men who has worked in the interest of the county, and indeed the country.

JOHNNY PATTERSON (1840 — 1889)

Johnny Patterson, famous circus clown and songwriter, was born in his father's roadside forge house in Kilbarron, near Feakle. His father was a nailer-gunsmith who was obliged to send his son to Ennis as apprentice nailer under his uncle Mark. Young Johnny's interest in music led him to enlist in the army as a drummer at the age of fourteen. One of the earliest songs Johnny Patterson wrote was about his youthful days in Ennis entitled, 'The stone outside Dan Murphy's door' — still popular even today. While in the army Johnny became an expert on both piccalo and drums.

After three years he bought himself out of the regiment and joined John Swallow's circus. He became famous as a clown in the circus but continued with his music and wrote 'The roving Irish boy' and 'The Dingle puck goat' during this period. He married another circus performer in 1869. Shortly afterwards one of his best known works appeared, 'The garden where the praties grow'. Patterson moved on to a number of other circuses and he was a national success by the age of thirty-five years.

His fame reached America and he was enticed out there to perform in one of the big circuses. During his voyage to America he wrote the song 'Goodbye Johnny dear'. He was billed as 'The Rambler from Clare' and was a great success until he returned when he was forty-five. In 1885 he went to live in Belfast and in 1887, Keely & Patterson put their own circus on the road. About this time a songbook was published in America containing many of Johnny Patterson's popular songs. It was about this time also that he wrote 'The auld turf fire'. During a performance of his circus in Tralee, a section of the audience mistook his symbolic wearing of the Harp and the Crown. As a result was attacked, punched and kicked, and a few days later, on 31 May 1889, he died. He is buried in the grave of a friend in Tralee.

HARRIET CONSTANCE SMITHSON (1800 — 1854)

She was a theatre actress who was born in Ennis in 1800. Harriet went to school in Waterford but at an early age she had to drop out and work as an actress to support her father who was ill. She gained much experience touring throughout the country. At the age of fifteen she played Lady Teazle in Sheridan's *School for Scandal*. She went on to Drury Lane in London where her strong Irish accent proved something of a hindrance, even though she was an accomplished actress at the time.

Macready's Company invited her to tour France with them, an offer she accepted. Her Paris performances became a great success where her brogue went unnoticed. Harriet Smithson met Hector Berlioz in Paris and they were married in the British Embassy in 1833. They lived in poverty — her fame was fading — and Berlioz was not yet successful. They separated in 1840 but Berlioz always supported her to the end. For the last four years of her life Harriet Smithson was paralysed. She eventually died at Montmartre on 3 March 1854.

SIR ERNEST HENRY SHACKELTON (1874 — 1922)

This man was born in a simple thatched cottage in Kilkee, Co Clare. He went on to become a famous explorer, making four remarkable Antartic expeditions. He was a member of Scott's expedition from 1901 to 1904 which got within one hundred miles of the South Pole. Shackelton commanded two more expeditions in 1907-09 and during 1914-16. In the former he reached 23 degrees south latitude and in the latter he was forced to abandon his ship, *The Endurance* in the Weddell Sea. He was knighted by the Crown for his exploratory work in the southern regions. Sir Ernest Henry Shackelton died on the ship *The Quest* on his fourth expedition to the South Pole.

THOMAS STEELE (1783 — 1848)

Thomas Steele was born at Derrymore House in east Clare on 3 November 1783. He went on to take a BA degree at Trinity College and an MA at Cambridge in 1820. After this he qualified as a member of the Institute of Civil Engineers. He inherited the family estate at Cullane but he developed a greater interest in restoring the castle of Craggaunowen. Steele fought at Cadiz in Spain against king Ferdinand. He had mortgaged his entire estate to raise £10,000 for the rebel army.

On his return to Ireland he joined with O'Connell in the great struggle for Catholic Emancipation, even though he was a Protestant. Together with The O'Gorman Mahon they protected the Emancipator from his personal enemies. Whatever little money he had left he squandered it on wild schemes until he was forced to go to London and work at engineering to earn a living. He was so distraught with poverty and remorse over the loss of his friend O'Connell that he jumped off Waterloo Bridge into the Thames. Although he was rescued he suffered severe injuries, and he died a few days later on 15 June 1848. He is buried in Glasnevin Cemetery, Dublin, beside his beloved Chieftain.

Bibliography

The History and Topography of the County of Clare, James Frost M.R.I.A., Sealy, Bryers and Walker, Dublin 1893. Reissued by The Mercier Press, Cork and Dublin, 1973.

The History of Clare and the Dalcassian Clans, Rev P White P.P., Gill and Son, Dublin 1893. Reissued by The Fercor Press, Cork 1973.

Statistical Survey of the County of Clare (1808), Hely Dutton, The Royal Dublin Society, 1808.

A full and accurate report of the trial of Cornelius O'Brien and Cornelius McDonough for the murder of Francis Drew. Printed by James Bryn, 1810, Dublin.

County Clare Pampletts, William Faussett, R.Y. Moffat and Co., Dublin 1867.

Inishcealtra Island in County Clare 1886, Richard R. Brash. An article in the Gentleman's Magazine & Historical Review, January 1866.

J.B. Scott's Property in County Clare 1856, Hodge, Smith & Co., Dublin 1854.

The Spas of Lisdoonvarna in County Clare 1856, James Apjohn M.D., Hodge, Smith & Co., Dublin 1856.

History of the O'Briens from Brian Boroimhe A.D. 1000 to 1945, Honourable Donough O'Brien, Batsford, London 1949.

A signposted walking tour of Ennis Town, Gerald O'Connell, with line drawings by Peadar MacNamara, Midwestern Regional Tourism Organisation Ltd., 1970.

A history of the Diocese of Killaloe, Part II-IV, The Middle Ages, Dermot F. Gleeson, M.H. Gill & Son, Dublin 1962.

Kilrush from olden times, James T. McGuane, Clodóirí Lurgan, Inverin, Co. Galway, 1984.

The Franciscans in Ennis, Patrick Conlon O.F.M., Athlone 1984.

Houses of Clare, Hugh Weir, Ballinakella Press, Whitegate, Co Clare, 1986.

Eamon de Valera and the Banner County, Kevin J. Browne, Glendale Press, Dublin, 1982.

Biddy Early, Meda Ryan, Mercier Press, Cork, 1984.

Worthies of Thomond, (Five Volumes), Collected and edited by Robert Herbert, *Limerick Leader,* 1944.

The war in Clare, Michael Brennan, Four Courts Press and Academic Press, Dublin, 1980.

History of Ennis Abbey, Thomas J. Westropp, Journal R.S.A.I., Vol XIX, 1889.

The Inchiquin Manuscripts, edited by John Ainsworth M.A., Irish Manuscript Commission, Dublin 1960.

The Forts of Limerick and Clare, T.J. Westropp, R.S.A.I. 1908.

Memoirs of the O'Briens, John O'Donoghue, Hodges, Smith & Co., Dublin, 1860.

Ordnance Survey Letters, Vol I & II, 1839. Vol III, 1841 John O'Donovan. Edited by Rev M. O'Flanagan, Bray, 1928.

General Guide to Clare Antiquities, Typescript in reference section, Clare County Library.

O'Brien People and Places, Hugh Weir, Ballinakella Press, 1983.

A Bibliography of Clare History and Antiquities, Maurice J. Flynn, bound typescript in Clare County Library, 1967.

The Diocese of Killaloe, Rev Aubrey Gwynn S.J., Dublin, 1962.

The Diocese of Killaloe from the Reformation to the close of the eighteenth century, Rev Canon Dwyer, Hodges, Foster & Figgis, Dublin, 1878.

Clare — County of Contrast, Seán Spellissy with photography by John O'Brien, published by S. Spellissy & J. O'Brien, 1987.

Survey of Megalithic Tombs of Ireland, Vol. I, Co. Clare, Ruardharí de Valera and Seán Ó Nualláin, Stationary Office, Dublin, 1961.

History of Clare Abbey and Killone, J. Power, 1987.

The Secret Places of the Burren, J.M. Feehan, Royal Carbery Books, Cork, 1987.

Long Ago by Shannonside, E. Lenihan, The Mercier Press, Cork, 1982.

Magazines:-
The Other Clare, Vol. I-XI, Dal gCais, Vol. 1-8.

MORE INTERESTING TITLES

IN SEARCH OF BIDDY EARLY
Edmund Lenihan

It seems certain that as long as Biddy Early is remembered mystery and argument will surround her name. She was a remarkable woman who possessed extraordinary powers and natural gifts of knowing the unknown.

The very mention of Biddy Early's name in any part of Ireland, especially in county Clare, releases an astonishing amount of stories about her cures, her magic bottle, her gift of prophesy and her many other curious talents.

The readers of In Search of Biddy Early can walk straight into the cottages of County Clare, sit by the hearth and hear at firsthand the stories passed down through the generations with the vividness and natural drama of all Irish storytellers.

LONG AGO BY SHANNON SIDE
Edmund Lenihan

Long Ago by Shannon Side is a heart-warming collection of colourful folktales and stories which were told around the turf fires in days gone by. There are stories about buried treasure, haunted places and strange meetings with the 'Good People'. We read about reactionary landlords, idiosyncratic priests and meet a host of local characters. Above all we see the people of Ireland at work and at play, in sorrow and in joy.

As every generation dies out part of their way of life dies with them. Already there is a whole generation of adults who have never enjoyed sitting by an open hearth in a thatched cottage listening to the old people remembering the way they used to live.

Jimmy Armstrong, whose tales these are, possesses the gift of storytelling usually associated with the seachaithe of long ago and his stories are guaranteed to entertain the reader.

THE FARM BY LOUGH GUR
Mary Carbery

The English born Mary Toulmin came to Ireland and fell in love with Lord Carbery of Castlefreke, County Cork and his Irish background. She learned the Irish customs and traditions and wrote about her adopted heritage. In THE FARM BY LOUGH GUR she records the memoirs of an old woman who spent her youth on a nineteenth century Irish farm.

This is the true story of a family who lived on a farm by Lough Gur, the Enchanted lake, in County Limerick. Their home, shut away from the turmoil of politics, secure from apprehension of unemployment and want, was a world in itself. The master with his men, the mistress with her maids worked in happy unity. The four little girls, growing up in this contented atmosphere, dreamed of saints and fairies. They lived in a rare world where the piper in the chimney corner piped jigs and country dances; the wandering fiddler played Mozart while the spinning-woman whirled her wheel; the old dancing master in knee breeches and velvet coat chasseed and pirouetted in his buckle shoes. Of course they had real problems and ambitions but their literal and dream world fused into a lovely background for growing, learning and loving.

The story is also a picture of manners and customs in a place so remote that religion had still to reckon with pagan survivals, where a fairy-doctor cured the landlord's bewitches cows, and a banshee comforted the dying with the music of harp and flutes.

THE MIDNIGHT COURT by Brian Merriman
A New Translation by Patrick C. Power

This is a racy, word-rich, bawdy poem; full of uncompromising language and attitudes which have earned it increased admiration and popularity since it was first composed by Brian Merriman in 1780. The bachelor uninterested in marriage and the aged bone-cold married man, the spouse-hunting lady and the dissatisfied spinster; the celebration of a woman's right to sex and marriage; disapproval of clerical celibacy - all these elements form part of the subject-matter of *The Midnight Court*.

Years ago, few speakers of Irish were without some knowledge of this full-blooded piece of literature, while very many people could recite the entire thousand and more lines of *The Midnight Court* in the version popular in their own area. It is one of the most interesting as well as entertaining survivals of the literature of Gaelic Ireland in the Penal times where humour, irony, literary tradition and sense of proportion had not fallen victims to oppression and humiliation.

The translation supplied with this edition of Merriman's poem is an endeavour to come as near as possible to the rural expression and attitudes which are part and parcel of the style of the original. Although actual use of dialect is avoided, the translator has used words and modes of expression occasionally which are found in English as spoken in the Irish countryside.

A Dual Language Book.

THE HEARTH AND STOOL AND ALL!
IRISH RURAL HOUSEHOLDS
Kevin Danaher

Most of the things which have become indispensible for us in our daily lives did not exist for our great-grandparents. Much of the work entailed by the absence of the labour-saving devices we know today would seem mere drudgery to us but was accepted as normal in their time. Against the drudgery we can set the fact that there was less noise, less dirt, less pollution, less stress and less fear.

In one thing they had a distinct advantage over us. They were more self-sufficient and independent. In their day to day lives they could provide for most of their needs. Many of them could build their own houses, raise their own food, provide their own fuel and control their own water supply.

By reading *The Hearth and stool and All!* you will be stepping back into the past and with a little imagination you will be able to call to life much of the spirit of the past.

BIDDY EARLY: THE WISE WOMAN OF CLARE
Meda Ryan

Nestled between the Clare hills and overlooking Kilbarron Lake stands a two-roomed thatched cottage, once the home of a notorious red-headed woman named Biddy Early. Arguments still persist as to whether Biddy was a witch or a person of God because she possessed powers and natural gifts beyond the comprehension of those who knew her personally. The very mention of her name in any part of Ireland, especially in County Clare, releases an astonishing flood of stories of cures, foretellings, warnings and broken spells.

Biddy's 'magic cures' were treated by the clergy with great suspicion as many priests believed that her power came from an evil source - the devil. In spite of life-long condemnations she was not intimidated by anyone and always took a firm line, respecting the clergy only in so far as they showed themselves deserving of respect.

Linked with fact, mystery and legend the fascinating story of the four times widowed, Biddy Early, will go on for ever.